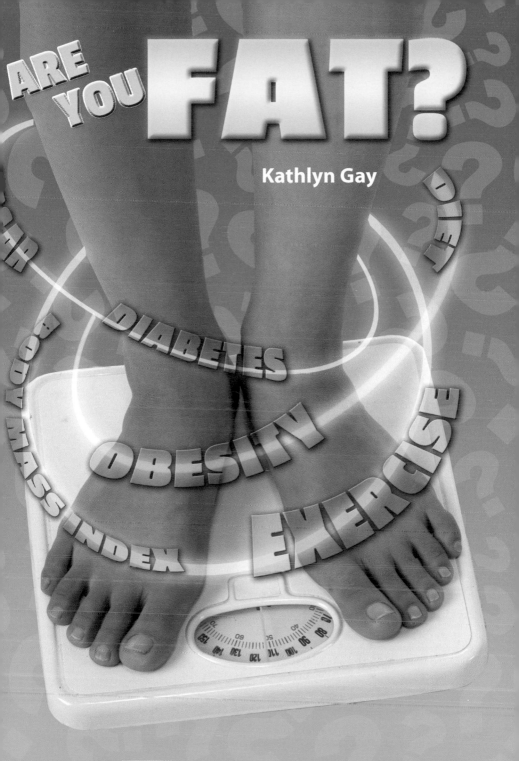

ARE YOU FAT?

Kathlyn Gay

DIET

DIABETES

BODY MASS INDEX

OBESITY

EXERCISE

E **Enslow Publishers, Inc.**
40 Industrial Road
Box 398
Berkeley Heights, NJ 07922
USA

http://www.enslow.com

Library of Congress Cataloging-in-Publication Data

Gay, Kathlyn.
[Am I fat?]
Are you fat? : the obesity issue for teens / Kathlyn Gay.
    pages cm. — (Got issues?)
  Summary: "Read about obesity, its causes, health risks, diets and their dangers, weight-loss surgery, and healthy lifestyles"— Provided by publisher.
  Revision of author's: Am I fat?, c2006. Includes bibliographical references and index.
  ISBN 978-0-7660-4322-0
  1. Obesity in adolescence—Juvenile literature. 2. Eating disorders in adolescence—Juvenile literature. 3. Teenagers—Health and hygiene—Juvenile literature. I. Title.
  RJ399.C6G39 2015 616.3'9800835—dc23

                              2013010593

Future Editions:
Paperback ISBN: 978-1-4644-0588-4   Single-User PDF ISBN: 978-1-4646-1284-8
EPUB ISBN: 978-1-4645-1284-1   Multi-User PDF ISBN: 978-0-7660-5916-0

Printed in the United States of America
062014 Lake Book Manufacturing, Inc., Melrose Park, IL
10 9 8 7 6 5 4 3 2 1

To Our Readers: We have done our best to make sure all Internet Addresses in this book were active and appropriate when we went to press. However, the author and the publisher have no control over and assume no liability for the material available on those Internet sites or on other Web sites they may link to. Any comments or suggestions can be sent by e-mail to comments@enslow.com or to the address on the back cover.

♻ Enslow Publishers, Inc., is committed to printing our books on recycled paper. The paper in every book contains 10% to 30% post-consumer waste (PCW). The cover board on the outside of each book contains 100% PCW. Our goal is to do our part to help young people and the environment too!

Illustration Credits: iStockphoto.com (FernandoAH, p. 19); Official White House Photo by Samantha Appleton, p. 79; Photos.com (Feng Yu, p. 5, FerliAchirulli, p. 72; IT Stock Free, p. 92; Joseph Abbott, p. 7; Peter Hart, p. 42); Shutterstock.com (Adisa, p. 57; Alila Medical Media, p. 64; ARENA creative, p. 15; Galina Barskaya, p. 31; Ivica Drusany, p. 7; Juliet Kaye, p. 38; michaeljung, p. 94; Milos Luzanin, p. 48; Monkey Business Images, p. 29; OLJ Studio, pp. 1, 50; Robert Davies, p. 24, Robert Kneschke, p. 53, s_bukley, p. 6; stefanolunardi, p. 60; Yan Lev, p. 87); Thinkstock.com (Photodisc, p. 84).

Cover Illustrations: Shutterstock.com/OLJ Studio

Contents

Acknowledgments 4

Chapter 1 What Is Obesity? 5

Chapter 2 Causes of Obesity 15

Chapter 3 Health Risks and Costs 29

Chapter 4 What About Weight-Loss Diets? 38

Chapter 5 More Diet Dangers 48

Chapter 6 Weight-Loss Surgery 60

Chapter 7 Who Is Helping? 74

Chapter 8 Healthy Lifestyles 87

Chapter Notes 97

Glossary 106

For More Information 108

Further Reading 109

Internet Addresses 109

Index 110

Acknowledgments

*Thanks to those who assisted with research:
Nissa Beth Gay, Gina Fontana, Shyam Dahiya, MD,
Amelia Barcenas, and Veronica Salotto.*

*I'm indebted also to those who shared
their experiences and views about obesity
in media stories and medical journals.*

What Is Obesity?

1

When Christianne was thirteen years old, she weighed 180 pounds, and faced daily taunts and jeers from classmates. "Kids at school called me stupid things like 'tub of lard' or 'fatty.' Some kids would yell 'moo,'" she told a Choices reporter, adding "It really hurt."[1]

Teenager Kendall Brasch, who weighed 265 pounds, said she had tried numerous diets to reduce her weight, but nothing worked, according to a report in the *Seattle Times*. In her words, "I was so depressed I didn't care about anything. I would go to school wearing pajamas, wouldn't talk to anyone and come home and sit in front of the TV."[2]

Like adolescent girls, boys also suffer when they are overweight and say it is clear to them that being fat is not acceptable to their classmates. They describe incidents of harassment, such as being called "fatty-fatty-two-by-four," "army tank," or "gun boat." One young man told of being picked on at lunch time, when others at his table threw food at him, calling him a "pig" and demanding that he eat the scraps or suffer a beating after school.

Whether male or female, some young people who are extremely overweight drop out of school and will not leave the house unless it is absolutely necessary. They may also be teased at home when brothers, sisters, or other relatives label them with humiliating terms: "fat chick," "orca," "big chops," and on and on. Early in their lives, they learn that those who are overweight are likely to be rejected. They become loners and have low self-esteem; they feel guilty because they cannot lose weight. Some say they reach a point where they hate to look at themselves in the mirror and dread buying clothes. Many teens tell about constant dieting or developing eating disorders in their efforts to control their weight.

On almost any given day, you can easily find a magazine or newspaper article, Internet posting, or TV news report that tells about the pain of children, teenagers, and adults who have been ridiculed, harassed, bullied, and sometimes physically assaulted because of weighing more, often much more, than their peers. In recent years, print and electronic media have also called attention to the health risks and economic costs of being fat—or in today's terminology: being overweight or obese.

Obesity

Although the terms fat, overweight, and obese are bandied about by the media, the words are not synonymous. In medical terminology, fat refers to the billions of fat cells in the body (40 billion in an average adult), and these cells affect basic body functions, according to the U.S. National Institutes of Health (NIH):

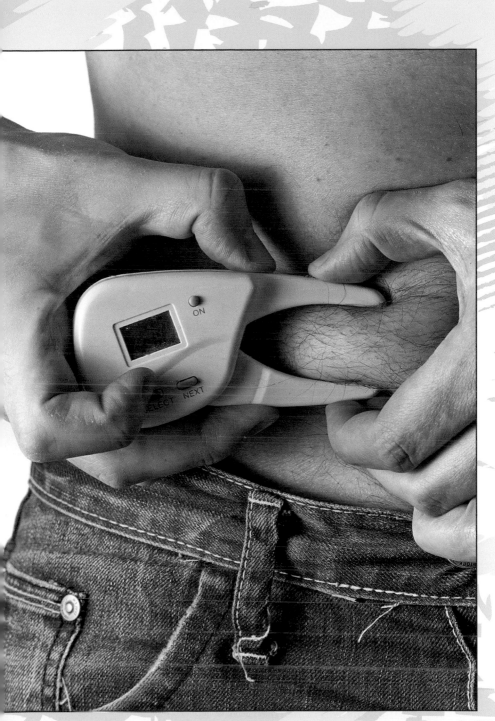

Calipers are used to measure the thickness of a fold of skin and the fat underneath it.

> Overweight refers to an excess of body weight compared to set standards. Excess weight may come from muscle, bone, fat, and/ or body water. Obesity refers specifically to having an abnormally high proportion of body fat. A person can be overweight without being obese, as in the example of a bodybuilder or other athlete who has a lot of muscle. However, many people who are overweight are also obese.[3]

A medical encyclopedia simplifies the definition, stating that obesity means weighing 20 percent or more than is considered desirable for a person's height, age, gender, and bone structure.[4] Such was the case for sixteen-year-old Amanda of suburban Pittsburgh, Pennsylvania, who was the subject of an *ABC News* report about obesity. Amanda, who weighed almost three hundred pounds at the time of the report, struggled most of her life with her weight. As she explained, "There was a time I gained twenty pounds in one month, and I was ten years old, and my doctor was like, 'Amanda, you can't do this.'" Amanda's father tried to help her by recommending diets and various programs advertised on TV. By the time she was twelve years old Amanda had been on numerous diets and had attended sessions of Weight Watchers, a popular program for losing weight. But nothing worked. As she put it, "I was always hungry."[5]

While the news report pointed out Amanda's and doctors' concerns, it did not indicate how she might eventually lose weight. There was little doubt, however, that unless she could shed pounds she was at risk for life-threatening health problems such as heart disease and stroke. She already suffered from diabetes and liver disease. Not only does obesity have adverse effects on health during the teen years, but obesity also can "extend throughout a lifetime if not checked," according to TeenHelp.com, and can be a risk factor for common health conditions such as:

• Type 2 diabetes
• Asthma
• Sleep problems, including sleep apnea

• Orthopedic (bone) problems due to an inability of the developing bones to support the excess weight
•Hypertension (high blood pressure)
• Heart disease

Additionally, teenage obesity can lead to psychological problems associated with negative body image and social issues associated with being treated as an outcast.[6]

Steady Weight Gains

Since the 1960s, Americans and people in other industrialized countries generally have been gaining weight, data shows. In fact, Americans are the second most overweight people in the world. The trend has steadily increased over the years among both genders, all ages, all racial/ethnic groups, and all educational levels. From 1960 to 2000, those considered overweight increased from 31.5 to 33.6 percent among U.S. adults aged 20 to 74. From 2009 to 2010, more than 35 percent of U.S. men and women and 16.9 percent of children were obese, according to a report from the National Center for Health Statistics (NCHS).[7] The Centers for Disease Control and Prevention put it this way: "More than one-third of U.S. adults (35.7%) and approximately 17% (or 12.5 million) of children and adolescents aged 2–19 years are obese."[8]

Similar increases have been recorded in Canada, although the levels are lower than in the United States. The NCHS reported "In 2007–09, the prevalence of obesity in Canada was 24.1%, over 10 percentage points lower than in the United States."[9] These extra pounds are leading to chronic diseases and literally killing people. In fact, the risks of death from obesity-related health problems could overtake death risks from smoking, analysts have predicted. The authors of an article in a 2009 issue of the *New England Journal of Medicine* noted that smoking among Americans has decreased, but "If past obesity trends continue unchecked, the negative effects on the health of the U.S. population will increasingly outweigh the positive effects gained from declining smoking rates. Failure to address continued increases in obesity could result in an erosion of the pattern of steady gains in health observed since early in the twentieth century."[10]

Body Mass Index

When health experts determine whether people are underweight, normal weight, overweight, or obese, they may use one of several methods. One is based on tables used for many years by insurance companies showing the desirable weight for one's height. Another is based on measurements of skinfold thickness, using calipers, a device that pinches the skin in various body locations, such as the upper arm, waist, and thigh. Calipers measure the thickness of a skin fold and its underlying fat, shown on a dial or digital readout. These measurements provide an estimate of the total amount of fat on a person's body. However, the accuracy of this method for measuring body fat depends on the skill of the person using the calipers.

The standard most commonly used to learn whether a person's weight points to a health risk is the body mass index (BMI). Someone with a BMI of 18.5 to less than 25 is at a normal weight and at less risk for an illness than those who have a BMI of 25 to 29.9 (indicating overweight) or those who have a BMI of 30 or more (indicating obesity). Generally, adults can figure their BMI by using a chart or a general formula.

The BMI has limits, however. Muscular people such as athletes may fall into the "overweight" category but not have health risks because they are actually fit. People who have lost muscle mass, such as the elderly, may be in the "healthy weight" category—according to their BMI—when in fact they may be at risk for various ailments.

When measuring normal weight for children and teenagers, the BMI standards are different from those used for adults. As children grow, the fat stored in fat cells and organs of the body change. For example, a child might have a high proportion of fat weight at age eleven but have a lower proportion by age thirteen as he or she grows

is table is for adults and is only an example of how BMI is determined. To use the table,
d the appropriate height in the left-hand column labeled Height. Then move across to a
ven weight (in pounds). The number at the top of the column is the BMI at that height
d weight. Pounds have been rounded off.

BMI	19	20	21	22	23	24	25	26	27	28	29	30	31	32	33	34	35
eight (nches)	Body weight (pounds)																
58	91	96	100	105	110	115	119	124	129	134	138	143	148	153	158	162	167
59	94	99	104	109	114	119	124	128	133	138	143	148	153	158	163	168	173
60	97	102	107	112	118	123	128	133	138	143	148	153	158	163	168	174	179
61	100	106	111	116	122	127	132	137	143	148	153	158	164	169	174	180	185
62	104	109	115	120	126	131	136	142	147	153	158	164	169	175	180	186	191
63	107	113	118	124	130	135	141	146	152	158	163	169	175	180	186	191	197
64	110	116	122	128	134	140	145	151	157	163	169	174	180	186	192	197	204
65	114	120	126	132	138	144	150	156	162	168	174	180	186	192	198	204	210
66	118	124	130	136	142	148	155	161	167	173	179	186	192	198	204	210	216
67	121	127	134	140	146	153	159	166	172	178	185	191	198	204	211	217	223
68	125	131	138	144	151	158	164	171	177	184	190	197	203	210	216	223	230
69	128	135	142	149	155	162	169	176	182	189	196	203	209	216	223	230	236
70	132	139	146	153	160	167	174	181	188	195	202	209	216	222	229	236	243
71	136	143	150	157	165	172	179	186	193	200	208	215	222	229	236	243	250
72	140	147	154	162	169	177	184	191	199	206	213	221	228	235	242	250	258
73	144	151	159	166	174	182	189	197	204	212	219	227	235	242	250	257	265
74	148	155	163	171	179	186	194	202	210	218	225	233	241	249	256	264	272
75	152	160	168	176	184	192	200	208	216	224	232	240	248	256	264	272	279
76	156	164	172	180	189	197	205	213	221	230	238	246	254	263	271	279	287

general formula to determine BMI is as follows: Divide one's weight in kilograms/pounds
height in meters/inches squared. Or another way is to simply multiply weight in pounds
703, divide by height in inches, then divide again by height in inches. Here's an exam-
. Suppose a person is five feet (60 inches) tall and weighs 120 pounds. Multiply 120
ounds) by 703, which equals 84,360. Divide that figure by 60 (inches), which equals
406. Divide the result again by 60, which equals 23.4, the body mass index. In this case,
e BMI is in the normal range.

urce: National Heart, Lung, and Blood Institute, "Body Mass Index Table," n.d.,
http://www.nhlbi.nih.gov/guidelines/obesity/bmi_tbl.htm> (June 20, 2005).

taller. Also, girls and boys differ in their body fat as they mature. So when determining BMI for children and teenagers, healthcare professionals frequently use weight-for-age growth charts, often called BMI-for-age charts (eight for boys and eight for girls).

Curved lines on a chart show percentiles, and a person's BMI plotted on the chart indicates whether his or her BMI exceeds or equals the percentage of others of the same age and gender. Suppose a five-year-old girl is in the fiftieth percentile. This means that 50 percent of girls of the same age have a lower BMI. If a fifteen-year-old boy is in the sixtieth percentile, this indicates that compared to other boys of the same age, 60 percent have a lower BMI. Whether female or male, youth in the age bracket two through twenty are considered overweight if their BMI is in the ninety-fifth percentile or higher, and underweight if in the fifth percentile or lower.

An Epidemic?

Health officials at the U.S. Department of Health and Human Services (HHS), the U.S. Food and Drug Administration (FDA), the NIH, and other federal agencies have been warning for years that obesity is a growing health problem for the nation and that there is an "obesity epidemic" rampant in the land. Most health care providers and institutions have echoed those alarms.

Yet not everyone agrees. The Center for Consumer Freedom (CCF), "a nonprofit organization devoted to promoting personal responsibility and protecting consumer choices," believes "the consumer is King. And Queen." The CCF argues that "A growing cabal of activists has meddled in Americans' lives in recent years. They include self-anointed 'food police,' health campaigners, trial lawyers, personal-finance do-gooders, animal-rights misanthropes, and meddling bureaucrats."[11] CCF also declares that "Countless studies have shown that physical inactivity, not certain foods and ingredients, is responsible for obesity....A narrow, food-only approach entirely misses the complex causes of obesity, especially physical inactivity."[12]

At the same time, some medical experts and researchers emphasize that a healthy lifestyle is more important than trying to reach an ideal body weight. Whether young or old, a person can have excess body fat and still be fit. "Thin people do not have a monopoly on health and fitness. Fit and healthy bodies come in all shapes and sizes," wrote Stephen N. Blair, Director of Research at the Cooper Institute for Aerobics Research, in a foreword for the 2002 book *Big Fat Lies: The Truth About Your Weight and Your Health*.[13] Blair has continued to argue "that being fat and fit is better, healthwise, than being thin and unfit," as a *New York Times* reporter explained in 2012.[14] Blair and others who advocate for exercise conclude that even though people may be in a high BMI group, they can still be healthy because they are active—they exercise and are not sedentary "couch potatoes."

Paul Campos, a law professor and nationally recognized expert on America's "fat war" also expressed an opposing view in his book *The Obesity Myth*. Campos wrote that the panic over obesity is unwarranted. He accused drug companies, medical professionals, diet-food manufacturers, diet gurus, and researchers of perpetuating concerns about obesity. Why? To earn more and more profits for the multi-billion dollar weight-loss industry.

Another opposing view was presented by Dr. Jeffrey Friedman in a *New York Times* article. Friedman is an obesity researcher at Rockefeller University in New York who discovered leptin, an appetite-suppressing hormone produced by fat cells. From his research, he concludes that body weight is determined by genes, which also control how much a person eats and burns food. In his view, the extent of obesity is being overemphasized in the United States with lots of misinformation circulating. As a result, Americans are made to feel guilty if they gain weight. He argues that a careful study of statistics show that while extremely obese people are increasing in weight, those who are thin are staying about the same. "Before calling [obesity] an epidemic, people really need to understand what the numbers do and don't say," he told *New York Times* reporter Gina Kolata.[15]

Debates over whether or not there is an obesity "epidemic" are not likely to fade away. Health experts are focused on the problem, although they acknowledge that the causes of obesity are not yet fully understood. As a result, numerous U.S. agencies and health professionals are continuing to investigate possible factors in the problem of obesity.

Causes of Obesity?

Factors that can contribute to being overweight or obese certainly include a person's genes, as Dr. Friedman argued. In fact, many scientists are focusing on the biology of obesity and are convinced that obesity is a disease. "Increasingly, researchers are demonstrating that obesity is controlled by a powerful biological system of hormones, proteins, neurotransmitters [electrical signals in the brain], and genes that regulate fat storage and body weight and tell the brain when, what, and how much to eat," according to a cover story in *U.S. News & World Report*. The story quoted Louis Arnonne, director of the Comprehensive Weight Control Program at New York-Presbyterian Hospital, who said "Once people gain weight, then these biological mechanisms, which we're beginning to understand, develop to prevent people from losing weight. It's not someone fighting 'willpower.' The body resists weight loss."[1]

Part of the resistance to weight loss can be linked to the fact that humans like other mammals have a built-in system that long ago protected them when food was scarce. Their bodies stored fat efficiently. When our ancient ancestors could not obtain sufficient food by hunting for meat and gathering fruits and nuts, they were still able to survive; their bodies used stored fat from food they ate during times of plenty. As humans evolved, they maintained their mechanism to guard against scarcity, but today with a steady source of food, most Americans do not need to store body fat for survival during times of famine. In addition, because of labor-saving devices and many modes of transportation, people do not use up body fat. As a result, individuals become overweight and obese.

Health-care professionals contend that the major cause of weight gain, overweight, and obesity can be summarized simply: people take in more calories than they burn up in exercise—sports, physical work, and other activities. Calories measure the production of fuel, or energy, produced in the body. When the calories we consume exceed our needs, the "extras" are stored as body fat. Caloric needs vary with individuals, however. "Average" teenage girls, for example, need only about 2,000 to 2,200 calories daily. "Average" teenage boys may use up to 2,800 calories daily. Teenage athletes or those who are very active, whatever their gender, could have much higher energy needs.

Cultural patterns, economic and social status, and emotional makeup also contribute to weight gain, other experts say. Some people, for example, may eat more than they need because food is comforting—it tastes good and may seem to ease loneliness, loss, sadness, stress, or anxiety. Young people may overeat because they are following a pattern set by their parents and/or their friends. Chronic diseases can also determine whether a person is thin, fat, or in-between.

One other factor connected to weight gain and increased BMI may be sleep deprivation—getting only five hours or less of sleep. Some people who are unable to sleep may get up in the middle of the night and snack, thus contributing to weight gain. But according to the long-term and continuing Wisconsin Sleep Cohort (WSC), a study of sleep disorders in which more than one thousand volunteers have been participating, researchers found that lack of sleep affects the levels of two hormones that control appetite: leptin and ghrelin. Leptin suppresses appetite and ghrelin stimulates appetite. Participants in the study who did not get enough sleep had low levels of leptin and elevated ghrelin—16 percent less leptin and nearly 15 percent more ghrelin than those who regularly slept seven to eight hours. In Western societies like the United States where people commonly have restricted sleep patterns and food is readily available, changes in the hormones that regulate appetite "may contribute to obesity," the study reported in 2004.[2] By 2012, the WSC was still underway and had received funds to continue until 2016.

Beyond the WSC, a smaller study was published in 2012 in the *Annals of Internal Medicine*. It also found that sleep deprivation can lead to obesity and diabetes. In particular, the study concluded that lack of sleep has a harmful impact on fat cells, reducing their ability to respond to insulin, a hormone that regulates energy. The study's author Matthew Brady, associate professor of medicine at the University of Chicago, noted that "Many people think of fat as a problem, but it serves a vital function. Body fat, also known as adipose tissue, stores and releases energy. In storage mode, fat cells remove fatty acids and lipids from the circulation where they can damage other tissues. When fat cells cannot respond effectively to insulin, these lipids leach out into the circulation, leading to serious complications."[3]

Lack of Exercise

Lack of exercise plays a major role in weight gain, experts say, and some health professionals insist that inactivity is the leading cause of obesity in young people. Two medical studies published in 2004 found that when overweight and obese children and teenagers engaged in vigorous exercise, they not only lost weight but also reversed damage to their arteries—damage that could lead to heart attack or stroke.

In one of the studies by researchers in San Diego, California, 878 adolescents aged eleven to fifteen took part. For a year, the young people kept track of their diet and physical activities. When researchers analyzed the data, they found that "insufficient vigorous physical activity," was the main risk factor for adolescent boys and girls to develop a high BMI. As Kevin Patrick, the physician who led the study, explained further, "Too much time spent...at computer games and watching TV may equal, or even exceed, diet... as important contributors to overweight in adolescence."[4]

In other studies, data from the CDC, showed that 77 percent of children aged nine to thirteen years participated in free-time physical activity during the seven days prior to the center's survey in 2011. Only 29 percent of high school students had participated in at least sixty minutes per day of physical activity on each of the seven days before the survey, and fourteen percent had not participated in sixty or more minutes of any kind of physical activity on any day during the seven days before the survey. In short, CDC declares that participation in physical activity declines as young people get older.[5]

The reasons for inactivity are manyfold. In some cases, families do not use available sports or recreational facilities and playgrounds in their communities because of safety concerns—fears about drug use, violence, bullying, or other threats. Or perhaps there are no parks, walkways, or bicycle trails nearby.

Studies show that teens who exercise regularly are less likely to be overweight. However, activity levels among young people have fallen in recent years.

Many U.S. families live in sprawling suburban communities where stores and other businesses are not within walking distance. People usually drive to get to their destinations, which contributes to an inactive lifestyle. Whatever the distance from home to school, U.S. teenagers are likely to drive and younger students are usually driven to school and other activities.

Another factor leading to inactivity is the growing number of students who avoid physical education (P.E.) or have little chance to take part in class exercises. School gym classes may be cut because of reductions in staff and funding, in spite of the fact that future health costs due to overweight and obesity may be much higher than the cost of gym classes. In many elementary schools, P.E. may be offered only once or twice per week. Only 28 percent of high school students took part in daily P.E. classes in 2003. Since then "there has been little increase in physical activity among high school students," reported a 2010 fitness blog, adding:

> A recent survey from the nationally representative Youth Risk Behavior Surveillance (YRBS) that gathered data from 1991 to 2007 found that enrollment in high school P.E. classes among white female and male students as well as Hispanic students in grades 9–12 did not increase or decrease significantly. And among black students, enrollment actually declined considerably. And indeed, across the board, minority students are less likely to be involved in sports and physical activities and more likely to engage in what researchers refer to as "sedentary behavior." Also, girls are generally less physically active than boys. As the age or grade level of students increases, their level of physical activity tends to decrease.[6]

As Dr. Patrick of San Diego concluded, watching television and playing video or computer games are other reasons young people (and adults) do not exercise. Kelly D. Brownell, a Yale University expert on eating disorders and obesity, cited study after study "showing that TV time is coupled with both obesity and poor food consumption in children and adults, males and females, and people across countries." By the time U.S. students graduate from high school, they "have accumulated more hours before the TV than in school, and this must be added to the hours people spend with video games and computers," Dr. Brownell wrote in his 2004 book.[7]

Time magazine reporter Alice Park noted in 2012 that "When it comes to being couch potatoes, Americans aren't alone." In her feature for *healthlandtime.com*, she wrote: "Physical inactivity has become a global pandemic, say researchers in a series of related papers published in the journal *Lancet*. According to one of the reports, lack of exercise causes as many as one in ten premature deaths around the world each year—roughly as many as smoking."[8]

Abundant Food Supply

While an inactive lifestyle and high calorie snacks and meals get a lot of blame for weight problems, some researchers point to the nation's food system as another contributor, directly or indirectly, to America's reputation as Fat Land (the title of Greg Critser's book on the subject). Over the past few decades, the food supply, the kinds of food, and the way people eat have changed considerably.

One major change can be seen in U.S. agriculture and the manufacture of food products. Even though many people believe that much of the American food supply comes from family farms of the "Old MacDonald" variety, that type of small family farm and family farms in general have been disappearing. Since about the 1950s, food production for the most part has become industrialized. Vast corporate-owned farmlands specialize in growing one type of crop or produce, or they concentrate on giant livestock operations (sometimes called "factory farms") that generate great quantities of meat or poultry. "The greater efficiency, specialization, and size of agriculture and food product manufacture have led to one of the great unspoken secrets about the American food system: overabundance," wrote Marion Nestle, professor and chair of the

Department of Nutrition, Food Studies and Public Health at New York University.[9]

Government subsidies have also contributed to the plentiful supply of processed foods. The federal government pays some farmers to raise such crops as corn, wheat, rice, soybeans, and sugar, prompting increased production and ever more food products high in calories. The relatively low cost of these foods creates intense competition among processors. Rather than raise prices to increase profits on competing items, manufacturers compete by introducing thousands of new processed food products each year. These products include many snacks, deserts, and sugary soft drinks that are high in calories and low in nutritional value, putting them in the category that dieticians and others label as junk food.

To sell junk food, companies aim a major portion of their advertising toward young people. The marketing begins with ads directed at toddlers and pre-schoolers. On youngsters' TV programs commercials peddle such products as sugary foods and soft drinks. Children who watch these programs are likely to see a food commercial every five minutes. One U.S. study that examined food advertising on TV programs aimed at children found that "food marketers are interested in youth as consumers because of their spending power, their purchasing influence, and as future consumers." Researchers noted:

> *On average, eleven of nineteen commercials per hour were for food. Of [564] ads, 246 (44%) promoted food from the fats and sweets group, such as candy, soft drinks, chips, cakes, cookies, and pastries.... The most frequently advertised food product was high sugar breakfast cereal. There were no advertisements for fruits or vegetables. Several other studies have documented that the foods promoted on U.S. children's television are predominantly high in sugar and fat, with almost no references to fruits or vegetables.[10]*

A report by Alice Park of *Time* magazine in 2012 discussed a study by Leah Lipsky and Ronal Iannotti, staff scientists at the

Eunice Kennedy Shriver National Institute of Child Health and Human Development. The scientists reported "that for every hour of television children watch, they are 8 percent less likely to eat fruit every day, 18 percent more likely to eat candy, and 16 percent more likely to eat fast food." Those results were published "in the *Archives of Pediatrics & Adolescent Medicine*, [and] shore up previous studies that have linked TV viewing with unhealthy eating habits among children." Park added:

> The reasons for the association aren't surprising: youngsters watching TV are exposed to more advertising for unhealthy foods, such as for fast food or sodas, than commercials for fresh fruits and vegetables. Kids who watch a lot of TV are also less likely to be active, and studies show they're more likely to prefer eating foods high in sugar, salt and fat even when they aren't watching TV.[11]

The Fast-Food Connection

Excess calories also come from convenience foods sold in stores and meals served at family and fast-food restaurants. Large-size frozen meals and packaged items such as macaroni and cheese in supermarkets, buckets of buttered popcorn at the movies, and super-sized soft drinks and sandwiches at fast-food establishments are common.

It is true that some well-known fast-food companies have started to serve smaller portions and lower calorie meals. As an example, McDonald's now offers salads and adult Happy Meals with salad, bottled water, and a pedometer to encourage walking. Other chains such as Wendy's and Burger King are also offering nutritious items such as milk, bottled water, or fruit juice that can be selected instead of sugary soft drinks; fruit cups and salads can be chosen rather than high-calorie, high-fat fries. Some chain restaurants offer "lite" or "low-calorie" sandwiches or pizzas that are lower in fat than their regular varieties.

Eating fast foods, such as burgers and fries is an easy and cheap way to add extra unwanted calories.

In 2007, Nickelodeon and the Cartoon Network adopted policies to restrict the kinds of food and beverage products that their characters use. And in 2012, Disney banned advertising for junk food on its programs for children. Years earlier, Disney had initiated a healthful-foods program in its theme parks in Anaheim, California and Orlando, Florida. That meant "including carrots and low-fat milk in children's meals unless parents request otherwise. Its consumer products division changed its licensed food program so that 85 percent of its offerings comply with the company's nutrition guidelines. Disney even chose to stop licensing its film characters for McDonald's Happy Meals, citing the link between fast food and childhood obesity," according to *Los Angeles Times* reporter Dawn C. Chmielewski.[12]

In spite of the emphasis on nutritious food, that does not mean that most teenagers worry about fast-food consumption. It is not unusual to hear teenagers say that they don't care about calories in colas or hamburgers and fries. They choose these items because they taste good, not because they worry about what is good for them. A study of 6,200 U.S. children and teenagers aged four to nineteen, published in *Pediatrics* found that on any typical day about one-third (30.3 percent) of more than 6,200 U.S children and teenagers aged four to nineteen ate fast food.[13]

Another study of teens aged thirteen to fifteen in fifteen industrialized countries concluded that "U.S. teens were more likely than those in other countries to eat fast food, snacks, and sugary sodas." This fact, claimed the authors of the study published in the *Archives of Pediatrics & Adolescent Medicine*, contributes to the rate of obesity among U.S. teens that is higher than the rate in fourteen other countries. However, Greece, Portugal, Israel, Ireland, and Denmark are not far behind the United States. Of the fifteen countries in the study, the rates for obesity and overweight are the lowest for teens in Lithuania, perhaps because there are not as many fast-food restaurants in Lithuania and teens do not have as much money to spend on snacks and fast food as their counterparts in other industrialized nations, one of the authors of the study reported.[14]

A different kind of study focused on teens thirteen to seventeen years old who regularly eat at fast-food restaurants. Fifty-four teenagers in the first part of the study were taken to a fast-food court and allowed to eat whatever they wanted. Secondly, researchers allowed the same group of teenagers to go to a fast-food restaurant of their choice: Burger King, KFC, McDonald's, Taco Bell, or Wendy's. "The participants were required to get one item with protein plus a side item, such as French fries or a soda," according to a news report. What did the researchers learn? On average, the teenagers consumed about 1,500 calories in fast food—more than half of their daily needs, but to offset the high calories, slim teenagers ate less later in the day, while overweight teens did not adjust their food intake and added about four hundred more calories to their daily fare.[15]

School Vending Machines

One more guilty party in the problem of overweight students may be the school vending machine, say many nutrition experts and government officials. To determine what vending machines offer for sale, the Center for Science in the Public Interest (CSPI) conducted a nationwide survey in 2004 of more than 1,400 vending machines in 251 middle schools and high schools. The CSPI found that 75 percent of drinks and 85 percent of snacks in the machines were of poor nutritional quality and usually high in calories. Common items were soda, imitation fruit juices, candy, chips, cookies, and snack cakes. With so much junk food in school vending machines, there is little incentive for students to make healthy food choices.[16]

A later survey concluded that "Three-quarters of middle schools have vending machines where snacks and sugared drinks are sold," according to Carolyn Colwell in a *U.S. News and World Report* article. Colwell cited a 2008 study of forty-two middle schools across the nation where researchers "discovered that most of these vending machines offer food and beverage choices that contain as much as 320 calories an item."[17]

Because of the studies, schools across the United States have been considering bans on or have restricted access to vending machines that offer junk food and sugary soft drinks. Some individual schools have removed sodas and candy from their vending machines. In some states students are limited to using vending machines and canteens at certain times during the school day. Other states require that at least half of all foods and drinks offered in vending machines in each school district include healthful items, such as granola bars, fresh fruit, 100 percent fruit juices, bottled water, and milk. While restrictions are more widely accepted today than a few years ago, outright bans on vending machines are controversial. Many teenagers, for example, believe they should be able to make their own choices about what they will eat and drink.

Arguments for vending machines also come from some school administrators and school boards who want to earn funds for their schools. How is that done? Soft-drink companies and other vendors provide beverages and snacks, and schools earn a percentage of the profits from product sales. According to an article in the *New York Times*, "A study by the National Academy of Sciences estimates that about $2.3 billion worth of snack foods and beverages are sold annually in schools nationwide."[18] The money schools gain from vending machine sales pays for sports programs and equipment, band uniforms, computers, and other "extras" that school administrators say they cannot afford because of cutbacks in tax funds allocated for schools.

Some school administrators are opting to keep vending machines but stocking them with healthier foods. The schools are responding to a federal law that President Barack Obama signed in late 2011. The law gives the U.S. Department of Agriculture (USDA) authority to require that all snacks and refreshments in vending machines meet the same nutritional guidelines set for school lunch programs receiving federal funds. Various firms such as Fresh Healthy, Vend

Natural, and Human Healthy Vending have installed machines with such items as granola bars, yogurt, and fruit smoothies. In addition "The biggest U.S. vending machine operators—Canteen, Sodexo, and Aramark—have started offering healthier food in recent years," wrote Nick Leiber in *Bloomberg Businessweek*.[19]

In spite of efforts to offer healthy choices in vending machines, some experts contend that vending machines may not be the culprits they are made out to be. They believe schools should promote weight loss with physical education and encourage healthy diets through nutrition classes. Others argue that beyond school classes, many more educational programs are needed to help the public understand the importance of nutrition and eating healthy foods, and what the health risks are for people who are overweight or obese.

Health Risks and Costs

3

Government agencies and health professionals who gather statistics and distribute information on obesity often emphasize the health risks for those who are obese. Along with all the studies and national data collected on people at risk, the costs of obesity are tabulated as well. These costs include medical expenses to treat problems that are linked to obesity. Illness and disease are the worst part of the obesity problem, but economic costs accentuate the hardship. Direct U.S. health costs due to obesity in 2008 dollars total about $147 billion, the CDC reported. The medical costs may include preventive, diagnostic, and treatment services related to obesity as well as income lost from decreased productivity, restricted activity, absenteeism, and bed days. There are also mortality costs— that is, future income is lost because of early death due to obesity related diseases.

According to the Weight-control Information Network (WIN), numerous diseases and health problems are linked to obesity. They include diabetes; cardiovascular problems (heart disease, stroke, and damaged blood vessels); gallbladder disease and gallstones; liver disease; osteoarthritis (a deterioration of the joints sometimes due to excess weight); gout (a disease that affects joints); pulmonary (breathing) problems, including sleep apnea in which a person can stop breathing for a short time during sleep; reproductive problems in women, including menstrual irregularities and infertility.[1]

Obesity is also linked to various cancers. Obese men are more likely than men who maintain a healthy weight to die from cancer of the colon, rectum, or prostate. Obese women are more likely than those who are not obese to die from cancer of the gallbladder, breast, uterus, cervix, or ovaries.

Diabetes and Obesity

The link between diabetes and obesity is of special concern, especially as an increasing number of overweight young people are diagnosed with the disease. "A total of 25.8 million children and adults in the United States—8.3% of the population—have diabetes," according to the American Diabetes Association (ADA). In addition "1.9 million new cases of diabetes were diagnosed in people aged twenty years and older in 2010." Of those under twenty years of age "215,000, or 0.26% of all people in this age group have diabetes" and "About one in every four hundred children and adolescents has diabetes."[2]

Exercise and a nutritious diet can help young people avoid the health risks associated with obesity.

Diabetes is a disease in which the body does not produce or properly use insulin, a hormone that converts glucose (sugar) and starches (like potatoes) into the energy that body cells need to function. There are two kinds of diabetes, Type I and Type II. Type I, once called juvenile diabetes, is usually diagnosed in children and young adults—their bodies do not produce insulin and they need several insulin injections a day or an insulin pump to survive.

About 90 percent of diabetics have Type II, and their symptoms may appear slowly as their bodies, for various reasons, fail to produce enough insulin or to use insulin efficiently. Type II diabetes was once an adult disease, but it has been rising steadily in all U.S. children, especially African-American, Hispanic-American, and American Indian adolescents, according to reports from clinics around the country.

A representative story about a teenager with Type II diabetes appeared in the *St. Petersburg Times* (now *Tampa Bay Times*) in 2004. It was about Jalisa, who has a family history of diabetes and was overweight. She was diagnosed with diabetes in 2002, when she was twelve years old, but at first she "wasn't really paying attention," she told a reporter. "I was ready to go back to playing and stuff with my friends."[3] And she continued to eat sugary snacks like candy and plenty of French fries.

Then Jalisa's doctor told her that she could suffer serious complications that could not be reversed. She needed to take care of herself: eat properly, take her medication to increase her insulin, and exercise. High levels of sugar in the cells can lead to such problems as damage to blood vessels and nerves in the legs and feet (requiring amputations) and blindness. Currently, Jalisa is careful about her diet, substituting healthy snacks like sunflower seeds for candy. She also exercises by riding her bike and walking. Yet, it's not easy for teens (or adults for that matter) to adjust to being diabetic. As Jalisa put it, "You miss out on a lot of stuff."[4]

In 2004, the National Institute of Diabetes and Digestive and Kidney Diseases (NIDDKD) of the NIH began a long-term, five-year study, enrolling 750 children and teens ten to seventeen years old with Type II diabetes. All were considered overweight or obese. The purpose of the study called Treatment Options for type 2 Diabetes in Adolescents and Youth (TODAY) set out to test diverse approaches to controlling blood glucose levels in youth and evaluate treatments so that doctors could effectively help young patients. Participants were assigned to three treatment groups. One group took a medication called metformin that reduces the amount of glucose the liver makes; the second group used a combination of metformin and another drug called rosiglitazone, which helps muscle cells respond to insulin and use glucose more efficiently. Group three took metformin and also was part of a lifestyle regimen for losing weight and increasing physical activity. Along with studying how each treatment approach controls blood glucose levels, the trial evaluated the costs of treatment and the health risks diabetic youth face.

The NIH reported in May 2012 that "A combination of two diabetes drugs, metformin and rosiglitazone, was more effective in treating youth with type 2 diabetes than metformin alone." In conclusion, NIH noted: "Further study will be needed to see if more aggressive therapy will yield long-term benefits for youth with type 2 diabetes as they move into adulthood. Another question is why the rigorous lifestyle intervention didn't bring the benefits that similar strategies have produced in adults. More research will be needed to design approaches that produce effective lifestyle changes for young people with type 2 diabetes."[5]

Metabolic Syndrome and Obesity

Nearly one million adolescents in the United States are affected by metabolic syndrome, a medical term for a set of characteristics that can lead to the early onset of diabetes and also heart disease. Researchers at the University of Rochester (New York) say that a young person who has at least three out of five of the following characteristics are at risk:

- high blood pressure
- high triglycerides (blood fats that increase the risk of heart disease)
- low HDL-cholesterol (HDL stands for high density lipoproteins in the blood that carry away the fat-like substance known as cholesterol)
- high blood sugar that can lead to diabetes
- abdominal obesity (fat around the waist)

The researchers reviewed data on 2,430 adolescents aged twelve to nineteen and concluded that at least 4 percent of all U.S. adolescents and 30 percent of all overweight adolescents met the criteria for the metabolic syndrome. Michael Weitzman, MD, professor of pediatrics at Rochester University, points out that "With this new information, when doctors see adolescent patients who are overweight, they will know to look for signs of metabolic syndrome, and to aggressively work with the patient to promote a healthier diet and lifestyle."[6]

Ethnicity and Risk

The burden of overweight and obesity is not evenly distributed across ethnic groups in the United States, and federal agencies try to determine which American groups are at risk for health problems linked to a high BMI. Groups are categorized by age, gender, race, cultural background, income, social status, and geographic locations. This is not an effort to humiliate or discriminate. Rather, it is one way to build awareness and encourage action to prevent obesity and the increased health risks associated with it.

In mid-2009, the CDC issued data on obesity, which showed that:

> Blacks had 51 percent higher prevalence of obesity, and Hispanics had 21 percent higher obesity prevalence compared with whites.... Greater prevalences of obesity for blacks and whites were found in the South and Midwest than in the West and Northeast. Hispanics in the Northeast had lower obesity prevalence than Hispanics

in the Midwest, South or West.... For blacks, the prevalence of obesity ranged from 23 percent to 45.1 percent among all states and the District of Columbia; among Hispanics in 50 states and DC, the prevalence of obesity ranged from 21 percent to 36.7 percent, with eleven states having an obesity prevalence of 30 percent or higher. Among whites in fifty states and the District of Columbia, the prevalence of obesity ranged from 9 percent to 30.2 percent, with only West Virginia having a prevalence of 30 percent or more. "We know that racial and ethnic differences in obesity prevalence are likely due to both individual behaviors, as well as differences in the physical and social environment," said Liping Pan, MD, MPH, lead author and epidemiologist. "We need a combination of policy and environmental changes that can create opportunities for healthier living."[7]

Poverty and Obesity

Money—or lack of it—can determine whether a population group is at risk for obesity and associated health problems. In the United States and some other industrialized nations, poverty and obesity often coexist. Although low income does not necessarily indicate that members of a family will have unhealthy diets or tend to be fat, numerous studies have shown that impoverished people are more likely to be obese than those of higher economic status.

"A significant body of scientific evidence links poverty with higher rates of obesity," Susan Blumenthal, MD for the *Huffington Post*. "Findings from the National Health and Nutrition Examination Survey (NHANES), the most comprehensive study conducted thus far to document the nutritional status of the U.S. population, has found that low-income children and adolescents are more likely to be obese than their higher income counterparts. Additionally, reports have shown a higher prevalence of obesity among low-income adults. One study revealed that more than one-third of adults who earn less than $15,000 annually were obese, as compared to 25 percent of those who earn more than $50,000 a year."[8]

Why are poverty and obesity linked? Part of the reason is that the foods a family can afford are those that are filling but high in calories. Nutritious, low-calorie foods like fresh fruits and vegetables, fish, and lean meat cost more than, say, a pizza or candy bar that eases hunger and provides quick energy but is high in calories. Another factor is that poor families often have limited access to nutritious foods or have little choice in the selection of foods in grocery stores. This is especially true in inner-city neighborhoods where there are few if any nearby supermarkets. Low-income residents frequently have to use public transportation to find a major grocery store, and returning on a bus or subway with bags of groceries can be extremely difficult. So the alternative in inner-city areas may be to shop at a neighborhood store which is sometimes a convenience store or glorified liquor store or eat at a nearby fast-food restaurant that offers large portions for a low price.

In many U.S. rural areas, families may have access to grocery stores, but poverty often prevents them from developing healthy eating habits. Regardless of rural or urban, "Communities are the cornerstone for preventive interventions that increase the accessibility of fresh foods and physical activity, implement policies to reduce the marketing of unhealthy foods to children and adults, and help make healthy nutritional choices easier and affordable," according to Blumenthal. "In this regard, public-private partnerships are critical in bringing families, businesses, health-care organizations, government and other stakeholders together to reverse the impact of obesity in our country."[9]

In some cities, efforts are under way or have resulted in establishing supermarkets in low-income communities and urban farmers' markets are beginning to accept food stamps. In addition, communities are working to create neighborhoods that offer opportunities for walking, biking, and more physical activities in general, especially for children and youth.

As many experts have argued, lack of physical activity is a major contributor to overweight and obesity and the costs that result.

Whether young people will get more active in order to maintain good health and avoid medical costs is a big question mark at this time. But it is certain that a great many adolescents believe that they are "too fat," and in their view not acceptable among their peers. So teens try dieting to lose weight or they wonder if weight-loss diets are for them.

What About Weight-Loss Diets?

Negative Calorie Diet. Sun Slim Diet. Ten Day Easy Diet. Slimfast Jumpstart Diet. Scarsdale Low-Carb Diet. Zone Diet. South Beach Diet. Atkins Diet. Sexy People Diet. Cabbage Soup Diet. Grapefruit Diet

Chances are you have seen advertisements for diets like these just listed. There are hundreds of them. They are frequently called "fad diets," which the University of Pittsburgh (Pennsylvania) Medical Center defines as an eating plan that:

promises quick weight loss through what is usually an unhealthy and unbalanced diet. Fad diets are targeted at people who want to lose weight quickly without exercise. Some fad diets claim that they make you lose fat, but it is really water weight you're losing. Fad diets that are restricted to certain foods may work, but most are boring or unappealing. This can make them difficult to follow on a long-term basis. And some fad diets can actually be harmful to your health.[1]

To control their weight, millions of people look for "quick fix" solutions such as all-liquid diets (which in most cases pose dangerous health risks) or diets that focus on eating a specific food. Consider the Cabbage Soup or the Grapefruit Diet. Eating just one type of food in unlimited amounts while eliminating items in other food groups is not nutritionally sound. Cabbage soup can be a healthy meal, but consuming it for most meals can cause gas and bloating. Grapefruit may help curb appetite before a meal or it can be a nutritious snack, but it has no special qualities to burn off fat.

Teens at Risk

Claims about the effectiveness of diets seem to be everywhere: on television, billboards, the Internet and in magazines, newspapers, and flyers. With all the recent focus on the dangers of obesity, teens may believe they should diet to lose weight or decide to engage in unhealthy eating regimens that lead to anorexia or bulimia. Anorexia nervosa and bulimia nervosa are serious problems that can develop among young people whether or not they are overweight or obese. Victims of anorexia have an intense fear of gaining weight and starve themselves, while people with bulimia eat but purge themselves of food by forced vomiting or by the excess use of laxatives. Both anorexics and bulimics place an abnormal emphasis on weight and body image and are usually secretive about their rituals. The disorders can have damaging health effects that can be long-lasting and even lead to death.

A University of Minnesota (UofM) study followed 1,902 teenagers and young adults who attempted to diet or engaged in unhealthy weight-control practices through several stages over ten years. At the beginning of the study, the participants had higher BMI values compared to those who did not diet or were not engaged in unhealthy weight-control behaviors. By the end of the ten-year study, the researchers found that "Persistent dieting and use of unhealthy weight control" practices increased the BMI of some participants. Adolescent girls in the study, for example, "increased their BMI by 5.19 units over the ten-year study period as compared with an increase of only .15 units among overweight adolescent girls who did not use any unhealthy weight control behaviors."[2]

Many teenagers who consistently diet, may try a fad diet that can put them at risk, preventing them from getting the nutrients they need for healthy growth, experts insist. The American Academy of Family Physicians provides some general cues on how to recognize fad diets, warning that you should stay away from diets or products if they:

• Claim to help you lose weight very quickly (more than one or two pounds per week). Remember, it took time for you to gain unwanted weight and it will take time to lose it.

• Promise that you can lose weight and keep it off without giving up "fatty" foods or exercising on a regular basis. If a diet plan or product sounds too good to be true, it probably is.

• Base claims on "before and after" photos.

• Offer testimonials from clients or "experts" in weight loss, science, or nutrition. Remember that these people are probably being paid to advertise the diet plan or product.

• Draw simple conclusions from complex medical research.

• Limit your food choices and don't encourage you to get balanced nutrition by eating a variety of foods.

• Require you to spend a lot of money on things like seminars, pills, or prepackaged meals in order for the plan to work.[3]

Teenagers often access the Internet for advice, but the safest course is to turn to the family doctor, a nurse, or a reputable nutritionist. Some questions a teenager or adult might ask are likely to focus on the popular low-carbohydrate (low-carb) and high protein diets and foods in supermarkets and restaurants. What are carbohydrates and proteins? They are nutrients that the body needs along with fat and vitamins and minerals. Carbs are the body's principal sources of energy and are found in starches (grains, rice, pasta, and potatoes), most fruits, and sugars. Protein is the basic substance of every cell in the body and is found in such foods as meat, poultry, fish, dairy products, and legumes.

Low-Carb Diets

Restricting the intake of carbohydrates is the basis for the popular Atkins Diet and also for the High Protein Diet, Hollywood Diet, Protein Power, South Beach Diet, and the Zone Diet, among others. These diets were developed in recent times, but long before they became popular William Banting, a carpenter and undertaker in England, wrote a booklet in the mid-1800s advocating a high-protein, low carb diet—a plan that he followed to lose weight. Since that time, developers of these plans claim that by eating foods low in carbs, the body automatically will burn more fat for energy and thus promote weight loss.

The Atkins Diet is the most widely used low-carb diet today. It is named for the late Robert C. Atkins, MD who published his *Diet Revolution* in 1972 and the *New Diet Revolution* twenty years later. Both books have sold millions of copies, and thousands of dieters claim success with the Atkins plan.

To "do Atkins," as the books and dieters refer to it, people severely limit high-carb foods—breads, pasta, fruits, sugar, and some vegetables. But the diet allows people to eat unlimited amounts of protein-rich foods and fat-laced foods such as butter, cheese, and mayonnaise. However, the diet has been controversial ever since it was first initiated. Some health experts consider the diet dangerous

Low-carb diets can be short on important nutrients, such as the whole grains contained in this sandwich.

because it limits carbohydrates the body needs and allows many protein foods that are high in fat content. A high fat diet can increase the risk for heart disease and obesity. In addition, a coalition of experts, argue that such a diet can:

> *force the body to use fat as its main energy source, resulting in 'ketosis,' a process that is jump-started by eliminating carbohydrates, and specifically glucose, which is what the brain needs for normal functioning. When faced with no dietary carbohydrates, the brain first causes the body to metabolize [change and use] the stores of carbohydrates in the liver and in the muscles and then to metabolize protein in the muscles, which can be converted to carbohydrates. With continued [reduction of] carbohydrate[s], the body converts to using fat and the brain is forced to use the metabolic breakdown products of fat, called 'ketones,' as the source of energy.*[4]

As this process begins, ketones are released in urine and dieters lose water, which usually results in weight loss. But as some dieters and health experts point out, lost water may be regained (along with weight) when people resume their customary eating routine. And many people do discontinue diet plans like Atkins because they are difficult, restrictive, and often expensive to maintain (Atkins, for example, requires dieters to take a host of vitamin and mineral supplements).

Controversy surrounding the low-carb Atkins diet plan has prompted medical studies to determine if its claims are valid. Early studies compared the amount of weight lost by severely obese individuals on the Atkins diet with weight lost by people following a more conventional low-fat, low-calorie diet. Researchers found that Atkins dieters lost weight more quickly than the other group, but by the end of a year there were no differences in weight loss. These studies concluded that in the short term low-carb diets can result in rapid weight loss (up to twenty pounds in a few weeks), but that there was not evidence that such diets are effective or safe over the long term.

However, in a 2010 book titled *New Atkins for a New You: The Ultimate Diet for Shedding Weight and Feeling Great* three medical professors declare that dozens of studies support the science behind the Atkins diet. The authors Eric C. Westman, Stephen D. Phinney, and Jeff S. Volek focus on eating more protein and vegetables. They argue that the updated Atkins program shows readers how wholesome foods can turn their body into a fat-burning machine.

Diet Programs

Other diet programs also make an effort to encourage a variety of food choices. Two examples are Weight Watchers and the Jenny Craig Diet Program. There are few if any forbidden foods, but dieters are expected to limit the caloric content of their meals. For example, Weight Watchers, which has millions of followers worldwide, uses a point system to help dieters determine their calorie count. Both programs have support systems: participants in Weight Watchers attend classes and meetings with other dieters; Jenny Craig dieters meet with a counselor once a week.

Drawbacks to these programs include the expenses for membership fees and meetings. For Jenny Craig dieters there are additional costs for prepared meals and vitamin and mineral supplements that they are advised to take. If dieters leave a program, there's another downside: they may be dependent on others to maintain a healthy eating pattern and fail to continue on their own without others' support or printed guidelines.

Although some overweight young people have tried Weight Watchers (usually because parents have advocated it), those aged ten to sixteen must have a doctor's referral and the signature of a parent or guardian to become a member. The program announced in 2003 that it does not accept children under age ten. Limiting access to children came about after "a thorough investigation into the state of the science in this area and found it to be almost uniformly disappointing," according to Karen Miller Kovach, chief scientist and global director of the program. "The methods deemed most appropriate for adults cannot simply be assumed to be appropriate for all children." She added: "I challenge anyone who currently says that they have a safe and effective weight-loss program for children to back up their claims with long-term data."[5] However, children between ten and sixteen can join Weight Watchers if they have a doctor's referral and signature of a parent or guardian.

Weight loss is rarely recommended for children under seven years of age. It may be appropriate only if the child's BMI falls in the overweight range and the child has a weight-related medical condition like high blood pressure or high blood cholesterol. Any weight-loss regimen provided to a child should be designed specifically for children and have a track record of lasting results. Adult-based weight-loss programs are not appropriate for most children.

Healthy Eating

Controlling one's weight in early adolescence does not mean pushing the panic button if there are sudden increases in body fat. Dieticians, nutritionists, and doctors stress that children's growth and development may happen in spurts. Before puberty, children gain some fat as part of the normal growth process. In early adolescence some may appear "chubby" for a time, but after they grow a few inches, their weight is appropriate for their age and gender.

In addition, the experts point out that whatever a person's age, it is important to be active and eat foods as recommended in the federal government's *2010 Dietary Guidelines for Americans*, which are online and can be downloaded.[6] The U.S. Department of Health and Human Services (HHS) and the USDA have jointly published the *Dietary Guidelines* every five years since 1980. Those guidelines were represented with a graphic called MyPyramid, but "In June 2011, MyPlate replaced MyPyramid as the government's primary food group symbol," according to the USDA. The department says "MyPlate is an easy-to-understand visual cue to help consumers adopt healthy eating habits by encouraging them to build a healthy plate, consistent with the *2010 Dietary Guidelines for Americans*."

The guidelines encourage people in the United States to eat foods and drink beverages containing less sugar and fewer calories. Keep total fat intake between 25 to 35 percent of calories for children and adolescents four to eighteen years of age, the guidelines advise. Most fats should come from natural sources such as fish, nuts, and vegetable oils.

Other key recommendations:

• Eat a variety of vegetables, especially dark-green and red and orange vegetables and beans and peas.

• Consume at least half of all grains as whole grains. Increase whole-grain intake by replacing refined grains with whole grains.

• Increase intake of fat-free or low-fat milk and milk products, such as milk, yogurt, cheese, or fortified soy beverages.

• Choose a variety of protein foods, which include seafood, lean meat and poultry, eggs, beans and peas, soy products, and unsalted nuts and seeds.

• Increase the amount and variety of seafood consumed by choosing seafood in place of some meat and poultry.

• Replace protein foods that are higher in solid fats with choices that are lower in solid fats and calories and/or are sources of oils.

• Use oils to replace solid fats where possible.

• Choose foods that provide more potassium, dietary fiber, calcium, and vitamin D, which are nutrients of concern in American diets. These foods include vegetables, fruits, whole grains, and milk and milk products.[7]

The guidelines also stress the importance of exercise, suggesting that children and adolescents engage in at least sixty minutes of physical activity every day, if possible, or at least most days of the week. Not only does regular physical activity help reduce weight but it also decreases risk factors for cardiovascular and other chronic diseases and improves a person's self-esteem and self-concept.

5

More Diet Dangers

When Kevin Zhou was a sophomore at Monte Vista High School in Danville, California, he posted an article in 2003 on *Online NewsHour* about the way the media covered teen obesity. In his view, the media had become almost obsessed with the story of obese teens and overlooked "the dangers of teens who will do anything to stay slim." He pointed out, "Pop culture has taught us that being skinny is good, and that being overweight is not. Students know that putting on too many pounds may put their social status in jeopardy." Zhou worried that the emphasis on the threat of obesity would cause those with "a solvable weight problem to turn to life-threatening ways of losing the extra weight."

Zhou was aware of the health risks of being obese, but he believed that "if news organizations want to report on teenage obesity, they should take up the responsibility of providing both sides of the issue and discuss anorexia and bulimia as well."[1]

Of course, most people who struggle to lose weight will not develop an eating disorder. But the continual blitz of media images that idealize being thin can trigger some risky behavior among those who think they are "too heavy" but in reality are an appropriate weight for their height, age, and gender.

Diet Pills, Supplements, and Injections

Fad dieting, as already discussed, is just one of the dangers facing those who are eager to be thin. Health risks may also come in the form of diet pills and dietary supplements, which include weight-loss products as well as vitamins and minerals and products that claim to treat everything from allergies to stress. Diet products and services are widely advertised and produce annual sales in the billions of dollars. In fact, diet pills and supplements plus weight-control programs, diet books, and health club revenues generated an estimated $58.6 billion in 2008, increasing to $60.4 billion in 2009 and $60.9 billion in 2010, according to Marketdata Enterprises, Inc., an independent market research firm that issues a study of service industries every two years.[2]

Sales pitches for diet pills and potions have taglines like "miracle diet pills," "herbal slimming pills," "weight-loss supplements," "fat-burner diet pills," "diet teas," "appetite suppressants," and "natural diet pills." Such terms frequently imply an almost magical method for losing weight. But do such pills and supplements work? An investigation by the TV program *20/20* found that advertisers sometimes use "misleading tactics" to promote the effectiveness of their diet products. Sometimes before-and-after photographs of people who provide testimonials for diet pills are manipulated or just plain phony. For example, a person paid to do a commercial might be told to gain weight and be photographed for a "before" picture

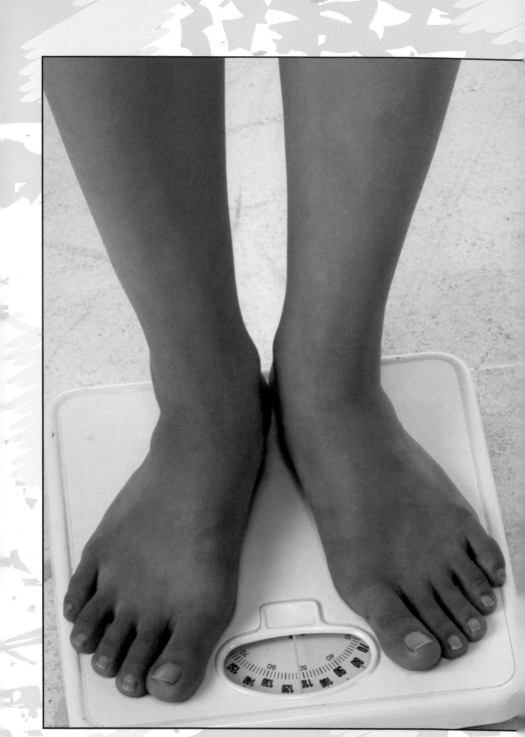

People with anorexia, an eating disorder, have a unrealistic view of their bodies and are obsessed with being thin.

and then take pills and work out to show weight loss in an "after" picture. One of the most serious allegations in the *20/20* program focused on the validity of medical claims. Some doctors are paid to promote a product in commercials but do not actually advise their patients to use it. The program advised viewers to use "a healthy dose of skepticism" when determining whether commercials for diet pills are based on fact.[3]

One of the latest weight-loss fads is mesotherapy, a procedure that involves many injections under the skin. The mixture injected may consist of medications, extracts from plants, vitamins, and chemicals. The solution is not standardized and doctors make up their own formula. Supposedly these injections help a person shed fat in waste products. Although mesotherapy has been used in Europe for fifty years, some doctors in the United States are concerned about its safety and doubt that the injections are effective at helping people shed pounds.

Rod Rohrich, MD, chairman of plastic surgery at the University of Texas Southwestern Medical Center in Dallas, give his opinion of mesotherapy on the Web stie *WebMD*: "This borders on medical experimentation," he says. "Injecting unknown substances into someone with multiple needle sticks is almost unconscionable." Rohrich adds "This is just another fad.... It preys on the consumer who wants to look for a quick solution, but there are no shortcuts to good health." According to *WebMD*:

That's what Leroy Young, MD, says as well. To Young, chairman of the nonsurgical procedures committee for the American Society of Aesthetic Plastic Surgery, mesotherapy is nothing more than "quackery." "There's just no proof that it works for any kind of fat," he says, adding that even those doctors who are in favor of mesotherapy advise their patients to eat well and exercise more. "If you eat properly and burn more calories, then guess what? You're going to lose the fat," says Young.[4]

Safety Issues

Whatever the diet products, you might assume that the products have been scientifically tested, that a government agency has placed its stamp of approval on them, and that warning labels for possible side effects are mandatory. But the Food and Drug Administration (FDA) uses a different set of regulations than those covering "conventional" foods and drug products (prescription and Over-the-Counter). According to the FDA:

> the dietary supplement or dietary ingredient manufacturer is responsible for ensuring that a dietary supplement or ingredient is safe before it is marketed. FDA is responsible for taking action against any unsafe dietary supplement product after it reaches the market. Generally, manufacturers do not need to register their products with FDA nor get FDA approval before producing or selling dietary supplements. Manufacturers must make sure that product label information is truthful and not misleading.... In addition, the manufacturer, packer, or distributor whose name appears on the label of a dietary supplement marketed in the United States is required to submit to FDA all serious adverse event reports associated with use of the dietary supplement in the United States.[5]

Sometimes dangerous supplements are manufactured and sold in the United States. Why? The case of the now banned weight-loss product ephedra provides one answer. Ephedra is also known as ma huang, a traditional Chinese medicine. Ephedrine alkaloids in the supplements are compounds found in the ephedra species of plants, and they have an amphetamine-type effect—like "uppers." The amount of alkaloids in ephedra-based supplements varies from product to product and an overdose can cause dangerous side effects—even death.

Before the ban, ephedra was widely promoted as the herbal equivalent of "phen-fen," short for a combination of the drugs

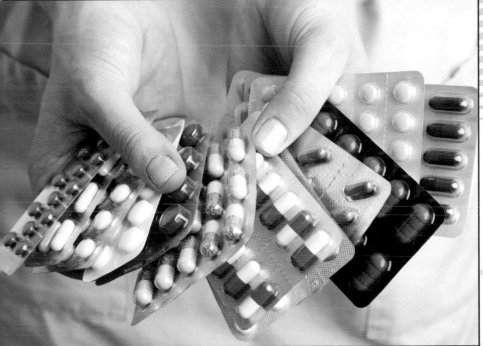

Teens should be skeptical about the claims made for weight-loss pills. Most are untested, and many are unsafe.

phentermine and fenfluramene, once used to treat obesity. However, "phen-fen" was banned in 1997 because of its connection to heart problems.

Beginning in the 1990s, the FDA issued warnings about the dangers of the stimulant ephedra in dietary supplements. But the federal Dietary Supplement Health and Education Act (DSHEA) of 1994 requires that the FDA show with certainty that any supplement on the market is unsafe before it can be withdrawn. Although the FDA has tried over the years to investigate consumer complaints about diet products, the agency has been unable in numerous cases to get sufficient information such as lists of ingredients or even samples of supplements. In some instances, the FDA has not been able to identify who manufactured products that users said caused adverse health effects. Nevertheless, reports continued to show ephedra-linked health problems related to the heart and nervous system, and the FDA finally banned the sale of ephedra in 2004, reporting that the product was "an adulterated food as well as an unapproved and misbranded drug, which present an unreasonable risk of illness or injury."[6]

The ban was challenged by some companies in the supplement industry, who argued that the herb *ephedra sinica* was safe and had been used for thousands of years as a Chinese medicine. A district judge in Salt Lake City, Utah, ruled in April 2006 that the ban could not be enforced. That decision was appealed to the 10th U.S. Circuit Court of Appeals in Denver, Colorado. A three-judge panel ruled in August 2006 that the FDA ban should stand and that the agency was correct in its assessment that the product was unsafe.

Internet Claims

Because many people (young and old) search the Internet for information on weight loss, they are especially vulnerable to suggestions that all they have to do is take a pill or potion and fat will fade away. The FDA reported that federal regulators "have found dozens of products being touted as dietary supplements but that actually contain hidden prescription drugs or compounds that have not been adequately studied in humans." An FDA spokesperson Michael Levy reported "These products are not legal dietary supplements. They are actually very powerful drugs masquerading as 'all-natural' or 'herbal' supplements, and they carry significant risks to unsuspecting consumers. We have seen deaths associated with these weight-loss products," adds Levy. "Make no mistake— they can kill you."

Some other safeguards that the FDA recommends when searching the Web include the following:

• look for potential warning signs of tainted products, such as promises of quick action... [or] "lose 10 pounds in one week"
• use of the words "guaranteed" or "scientific breakthrough"
• labeled or marketed in a foreign language
• marketed through mass e-mails
• marketed as an herbal alternative to an FDA-approved drug or as having effects similar to prescription drugs

In addition, the FDA advises consumers who use or plan to use dietary supplements to:
• check with your health care professional or a registered dietitian about any nutrients you may need in addition to your regular diet
• ask your health care professional for help distinguishing between reliable and questionable information
• ask yourself if it sounds too good to be true
• be cautious if the claims for the product seem exaggerated or unrealistic
• watch out for extreme claims such as "quick and effective" or "totally safe"
• be skeptical about anecdotal information from personal "testimonials" about incredible benefits or results obtained from using a product.[7]

Buyer Beware

Beyond being cautious about Internet claims and information, there are still other places where a person seeking weight-loss or diet products should be wary: in grocery stores and restaurants. While a decade ago many Americans were buying low-fat foods for weight loss and "heart healthy" diets, today there is a trend (some call it a "craze") for low-carb items—low-carb bagels, low-carb brownies, low-carb taco shells, low-carb-you-name-it. Hundreds of low-carb products are on the market, and costs of commercially packaged low-carb products are usually higher than, say, "regular" bagels or brownies.

Labels on packaged low-carb foods may claim they are "0% carb," "low-carb," "reduced carb," "carb smart," or some other slogan that appeals to dieters. Some marketers are touting products like meat or fish as "no-carb," even though they never had carbohydrates in them. Or they repackage products as "low carb" that have been sold for many years simply as diet foods. In short, a low-carb label "is not what it seems," states the University of California Berkeley *Wellness Letter*. "And any benefits these foods might offer for weight loss or nutrition are debatable, at best. If you replace carbohydrates with protein (that's the main change), you still have just as many calories. Furthermore, the labels are, essentially, meaningless. The FDA has no definition of 'low-carbohydrate' and has never approved any low-carb labels. Any food can be so labeled." The *Letter* ends with this advice: "Don't be fooled by low-carb foods. There's no evidence that they'll help you lose weight. They are not significantly more nutritious or less caloric than many regular foods. And they eat up food dollars better spent on plain good healthy foods such as fresh fruits and vegetables."[8]

Some fast-food and family restaurants are also on the low-carb bandwagon. McDonald's, Burger King, Wendy's, Subway, Ruby Tuesday's, and TGI Friday's are among the well-known chains hyping low-carb meals. But as with packaged foods, low-carb meals

The USDA recommends choosing from a wide variety of nutritious foods and limiting portion sizes in order to lose weight.

may not be as healthy as some regular fare. In some cases there are more calories and fat in the meals than described on the menu, because the size of the meal or item and amount of ingredients were larger than expected. Portions often depend on the judgment of the person preparing the food—or on the person ordering from a menu.

Because Americans increasingly eat restaurant meals or other food away from home, the U.S. Congress passed a law in 2010 that requires chain restaurants with twenty or more outlets to post the number of calories in their menu items. The law also requires that the chains include nutrition information. For example, a McDonald's menu shows that a caesar salad with grilled chicken has 190 calories, 5 grams of fat, 10 grams of carbs, and 27 grams of protein. A grilled chicken breast at KFC contains 220 calories, 7 grams of fat, 0 carbs, and 40 grams of protein. There are 230 calories in a soft taco supreme at Taco Bell and 22 grams of carbs along with 10 grams of protein.

In spite of the food labeling requirements for fast-food items, teenagers do not pay much attention to the calories and nutritional information. Calorie counters are more likely to be women and people living in high-income neighborhoods. If cost is an issue, a promotion for a foot-long Subway sandwich priced at five dollars takes precedence over an item that might be lower in calories and more nutritious.

Nutrition expert Marion Nestle responded to questions about whether calories really do count in a 2012 feature for the *San Francisco Chronicle*. Her answer: "Calories matter for weight. The choice of foods that provide the calories matters a lot for health and may make it easier for you to diet successfully. To lose weight, reducing calorie intake below expenditure [what you use up] works every time." Nestle pointed out that people can lose weight on low-carb, high-fat diets, but, she cautioned, "Most studies of extreme diets of any type report high dropout rates or failure to stick to the diet for more than six months or so. And even though initial weight loss is rapid on low-carbohydrate diets because of water loss, these diets are low in fiber and some vitamins." In conclusion, she noted, "The greatest challenge in dieting is to figure out how to eat less— and to eat healthfully on a regular basis—in the midst of today's 'eat more' food environment."[9]

Rather than eating more just because the food is there and on a menu, it is possible to make healthy choices while at a restaurant. USDA guidelines suggest when eating out, choose a smaller size option (for example, a small appetizer). "Manage larger portions by sharing or taking home part of your meal. Check posted calorie counts or check calorie counts online before you eat at a restaurant." Also "choose dishes that include vegetables, fruits, and/or whole grains…. avoid choosing foods with the following words: creamy, fried, breaded, battered, or buttered. In addition, keep portions of syrups, dressings, and sauces small."[10]

Of course, it is not always possible or practical to measure portions when eating out, and most of us misjudge the amount of food or beverage we consume, which could easily result in taking in more calories than expected. But those who want to eat smaller servings can keep in mind everyday items to help determine whether they are eating healthy food portions and keeping their calories low. Some examples: ½ cup of ice cream is about the size of a tennis ball; a recommended serving of chicken breast or lean meat is similar in size to a deck of cards or the palm of one's hand; vegetable servings may be the size of a baseball. In short, for a healthy diet the recommended portion size has to be considered along with the number of calories and the nutrient content of foods and beverages.

6

Weight-Loss Surgery

In spite of efforts to avoid fad diets, follow a healthy eating plan, and increase activity, some people simply do not lose weight. Indeed that has been true for numerous adults and young people who are classified as morbidly obese. What is morbid obesity? The term is applied to those who are extremely overweight—one hundred pounds over their ideal body weight. However, "the accepted definition currently is by BMI, which has to be forty or above if obesity is the only problem," says Shyam Dahiya, MD, who specializes in surgical treatment of the morbidly obese at the Bellflower Medical Center in Southern California. He adds that people "may be seen as morbidly obese if they have a BMI of thirty-five or higher and also have obesity-related health problems such as sleep apnea (disturbed breathing that interrupts sleep), hypertension (high blood pressure), or Type II diabetes."[1]

Someone who is severely obese may suffer from a chronic condition in which symptoms of the problem build slowly. Morbid obesity is then difficult (and sometimes impossible) to treat through diet and exercise alone. After many attempts to lose weight, some morbidly obese people seek a last resort: bariatric surgery, more commonly called weight-loss surgery. The term bariatric stems from Greek words meaning "weight" and "treatment."

Bariatric Surgery

Bariatric surgery has been practiced for several decades, and the number of such surgeries has been increasing steadily over the years. Currently about 200,000 bariatric surgeries are performed each year. One reason for the large number of surgeries is the publicity generated by TV personalities, such as singer Carnie Wilson and Al Roker, a popular weatherman and well-known food lover. Both Wilson and Roker once weighed more than three hundred pounds and had gastric bypass surgery. Within months, they lost substantial weight, and their experiences were widely publicized.

Gastric bypass is the most common weight-loss surgery, and involves creating a small stomach pouch and "bypassing" the lower stomach by connecting the pouch directly to the small intestine. Until recent times, this surgery required making a large incision (cut), dividing skin and muscle in the abdomen. Today specialists use a less invasive procedure called laparoscopy, from the Greek words meaning "look into the abdomen." Surgeons use a laparoscope, a pencil-thin optical telescope, inserting it into the abdomen through a small incision. The lightweight, high-resolution video camera allows surgeons to see into the abdomen, explore the whole cavity, and perform the necessary procedures.

Wendy Wilson, Chynna Phillips, and Carnie Wilson perform at the "Wilson Phillips: Still Holding" launch party and CD signing, Loehmann's, Beverly Hills, California on April 15, 2012. In January 2012, Wilson underwent weight-loss surgery a second time—this time lap-band surgery. By April, 2012, she had lost thirty pounds.

Following surgery, a patient achieves the best results when she or he establishes a healthy eating pattern and engages in regular exercise and other physical activities. As the Bellflower Medical Center makes clear, the weight-loss program "is about much more than surgery. It's about a lifelong commitment to a healthier lifestyle."[2] Along with surgeons, specialists from dieticians to physical therapists make up a team at the center that provides direction and support such as nutritional education, meal planning, and exercise guidance for patients.

Another type of bariatric surgery is called lap-band surgery in which a silicone band is placed around the stomach and decreases the stomach to about the size of an egg so that a person is able to eat less food. The procedure also may rearrange the small intestine so the body absorbs fewer calories. One side effect of weight-loss surgery occurs when patients eat sugary or high-carbohydrate foods. They may experience what is known as the "dumping syndrome"— they feel nauseous, get sweaty, and suffer from diarrhea. Sometimes called the "postop cop," the syndrome helps patients lose weight by discouraging the intake of high-calorie foods and beverages or simply too much food.

Yet, sometimes bariatric surgery does not prevent a person from gaining weight again. That happened to singer Carnie Wilson who once weighed 300 pounds and dropped to 150 pounds after gastric by-pass surgery in 1999, which was televised. Later, she wrote two books about her experiences. But in January 2012, she underwent weight-loss surgery again—this time lap-band surgery. By April 2012 she had lost thirty pounds. She "is now a paid spokesperson for Allergan, the company that developed the lap-band procedure she had," reported JoNel Aleccia of *NBC News*. Aleccia noted "There are no statistics about the number of people who get two or more weight-loss surgeries," but apparently it is rare.[3]

Currently, surgeons can use laparoscopic techniques to implant an adjustable gastric band. *WebMD* explains:

Gastric banding surgery involves the following:

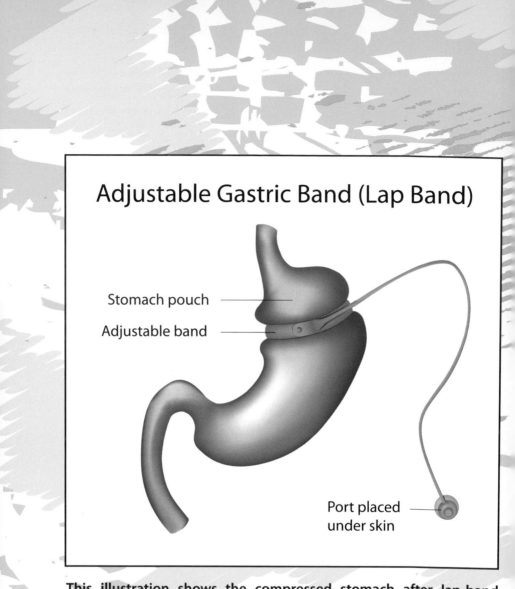

Adjustable Gastric Band (Lap Band)

Stomach pouch

Adjustable band

Port placed
under skin

This illustration shows the compressed stomach after lap-band surgery.

• Using laparoscopic tools, the surgeon places an adjustable silicone band around the upper part of the stomach.

• Squeezed by the silicone band, the stomach becomes a pouch with about an inch-wide outlet. After banding, the stomach can only hold about an ounce of food.

• A plastic tube runs from the silicone band to a device just under the skin. Saline (sterile salt water) can be injected or removed through the skin, flowing into or out of the silicone band. Injecting saline fills the band and makes it tighter.

• In this way, the band can be tightened or loosened as needed. This can reduce side effects and improve weight loss.

Laparoscopic adjustable gastric banding leads to loss of about 40 percent of excess weight, on average. For example, someone who is two hundred pounds overweight could expect to lose an average of eighty pounds after gastric banding. However, these results vary widely.

Gastric banding is considered the least invasive weight loss surgery. It is also the safest. The procedure can be reversed if necessary, and in time, the stomach generally returns to its normal size.[4]

An experimental procedure to treat overweight patients is a device known as a gastric pacemaker, which is available in Europe but has not yet been approved for use in the United States. Currently, the only gastric pacemaker that the FDA has approved is a device that treats gastroparesis, a chronic disorder that includes symptoms such as bloating, nausea, and vomiting. To treat obesity with the pacemaker, a surgeon attaches electrodes to the stomach wall. A wire connects electrodes to the pacemaker—a stimulator that is about the size of a silver dollar. The pacemaker is implanted under the skin in the abdomen and sends electrical currents to the stomach. It is not certain exactly what the stimulation does, but researchers say the device may activate hormones that help patients feel full and thus they eat less. Studies on the gastric pacemaker are continuing to determine how the device triggers hormones and what effect they have on weight loss.

Teens and Weight-loss Surgery

While numerous adults have had gastric bypass surgery over the past decade, that is not the case for adolescents who are still growing. Usually doctors do not recommend weight-loss surgery for an obese teen unless the young person has obtained full skeletal and sexual growth and might already be suffering adult problems such as arthritis, diabetes, and high blood pressure. According to the Weight-control Information Network: "Experts in childhood obesity and bariatric surgery suggest that families consider surgery only after youth have tried for at least six months to lose weight and have not had success." WIN says adolescent candidates should be extremely obese (with a BMI over forty), have reached their adult height, and suffer "serious health problems linked to weight, such as type 2 diabetes or sleep apnea, that may improve with bariatric surgery." In addition, WIN declares:

> health-care providers should assess potential patients and their parents to see how emotionally prepared they are for the surgery and the lifestyle changes they will need to make. Health-care providers should also refer young patients to special youth bariatric surgery centers that focus on meeting the unique needs of youth.
>
> Mounting evidence suggests that bariatric surgery can favorably change both the weight and health of youth with extreme obesity. Over the years gastric bypass surgery has been the main operation used to treat extreme obesity in youth.[5]

Veronica Salotto of Bellflower, California, is an example. At the age of nineteen, she underwent laparoscopic surgery with Dr. Dahiya performing the operation. Veronica explained that she had been overweight since early childhood and when she bought clothes they had to be the larger sizes. In her words, "At the age of eight, I was wearing about a size twelve in the women's sizes. Going

Television personality and weatherman Al Roker has had weight-loss surgery.

to school wasn't very much fun because not only did I realize I was different but so did my classmates."

Veronica's mother was also overweight and had bariatric surgery in 2002. Her mother suggested that surgery might also help her daughter. As Veronica reports:

> At first I was skeptical, but I began researching a little myself to understand what this surgery was really about. As my mom was going through the pre-operational doctor visits, we attended a few support group meetings. After seeing and hearing so many success stories, I began to realize that this type of surgery might be really good for me.

At the age of seventeen, Veronica decided to meet with Dr. Dahiya, and afterward came to the conclusion that she was too young to make the decision about surgery and was not ready for the procedure. But, she reports, "two years and frequent doctor visits later, I was well prepared and ready for this. Everything was cleared, and I had my surgery August 9, 2004.... This surgery has given me a second chance on my life.... I am thankful that I am alive, and I am even more thankful to know that I will be alive much longer than I thought I would be."[6]

Teenager Amanda Rodriguez of Hialeah, Florida, is another example. When she was in high school, she weighed 292 pounds and for two years had tried diets and various exercise regimens to lose weight. But nothing worked. She could not climb the stairs at school and had to use the staff elevator to get to classes. She suffered from depression, had high blood pressure, and was prediabetic. "I knew I was really unhealthy. I was in pain all the time, physically and emotionally," she told reporter Irene Maher of the *Tampa Bay Times*. Amanda and her parents were convinced that bariatric surgery was the only option. After her 2009 surgery, she lost 122 pounds, but maintaining the weight loss has not been easy. As Maher reported:

As careful as [Rodriguez] tries to be, it doesn't take much to upset her system. She still can't eat and drink at the same meal without becoming ill, and has suffered a number of 'dumping' episodes. She must wait a full hour after eating before taking a few sips of water, or she becomes ill.[7]

In 2012, Rodriguez was a student at the University of Connecticut and noted that "I'm able to walk around the campus and I'm able to go on school field trips and kind of interact with really cute guys," she told Diana Gonzalez of *NBC News.*[8]

A number of media outlets have featured teens who have had successful weight-loss surgeries. Why are they in the news? Until early in 2004, only about a dozen hospitals in the United States had bariatric surgery programs for teens. But because of long-term health risks for morbidly obese youth, more hospitals have considered such programs or have started them. Before teenagers are accepted for surgery, however, they are screened by health professionals to make sure that they have tried dieting, exercising, and other measures before undergoing weight-loss surgery.

In spite of precautions, not all doctors are convinced that bariatric surgery is right for teens. Some point out that teenagers are not dropping dead from obesity and that diet and exercise should take priority. Skeptics contend that there is no guarantee that teen surgeries will be successful just because adults have fared well. Doubters are also concerned about whether teenagers are disciplined enough after surgery to keep up an exercise program and stay away from junk food and other high-calorie items that can stretch the stomach—and add weight. A patient's family has to be willing to be part of the follow-up, which lasts years, helping a young person modify his or her behavior and maintain healthy eating habits and physical activities. Without this family support, the weight-loss surgery cannot be successful, doctors say. Still other critics question whether teenagers who have bariatric surgery will get enough nutrients in the small amount of food they can eat daily.

Lack of nutrients could affect growth and learning and perhaps lead to osteoporosis (brittle bones) because of calcium deficiencies.

The Costs

Whether for teenagers or adults, bariatric surgery can be expensive, and the cost can be a significant factor in whether or not the operation takes place. The estimated cost of the operation ranges from about $17,000 to $30,000. After surgery, there can be additional expenses for years of continued care. Although young patients see reductions in their health-care costs, older bariatric surgery patients are not as fortunate, a study released in 2012 indicates. Published in the *Archives of Surgery*, the study of patients in twelve Veterans Administration medical centers found that three years after the procedure "bariatric surgery does not appear to be associated with reduced health care expenditures."[9] One of the study's authors indicated that another follow-up study of the veterans would be made to determine if after five or six years their health-care costs are reduced, according to a *New York Times* blog.[10]

In some cases, health insurance plans, including those of Medicare and Medicaid, pay for bariatric surgery, particularly if it is medically necessary—that is, the patient's BMI is forty or above or the patient is severely overweight and has life-threatening health problems such as heart disease. Yet, insurance coverage varies, and it is not unusual for some insurance companies to turn down patients who want the surgery but are on the borderline of being morbidly obese (for example, someone who has a BMI of thirty-nine).

Some insurance companies will not cover bariatric surgery no matter what the conditions, citing various reasons such as the possibility of medical complications. There are also concerns that an increasing number of doctors entering the field of bariatric surgery have little experience or may not be adequately trained. Indeed, some surgeons qualified in other procedures, simply announce that they will perform bariatric surgery even though they have little or no training in that area.

Weight-Loss Surgery

"Bariatric surgery is not a specialty certified by the American Board of Surgery or other medical bodies," according to *American Medical News (AMNews)*. A doctor certified as a surgeon can enroll in a bariatric seminar or course at a bariatric center, hospital, or institute. "The level of training received by surgeons varies widely, from experiences in residencies or full-fledged yearlong fellowships to weeklong mini-fellowships or brief preceptorships [educational programs] taught by experienced weight-loss surgeons."[11]

What About Liposuction?

Liposuction is another type of surgery that technically is part of bariatric medicine, which is concerned with all methods of weight loss. Liposuction is a surgical procedure in which adipose tissue under the skin, which contains fat cells, is broken up and sucked out with a vacuum-like instrument. About 400,000 such procedures are performed each year, primarily for cosmetic purposes—to lose flab around the waist, upper arms, buttocks, hips, and other areas.

Over the years, plastic surgeons who have performed liposuction have touted their procedure as a treatment for obesity, believing it would lower risks for diabetes and heart disease. But a study published in the *New England Journal of Medicine* showed that liposuction does not affect these risks. The study was led by Samuel Klein, MD, director of the Center for Human Nutrition at the Washington University School of Medicine in St. Louis, Missouri.

Klein and other researchers expected that removing large amounts of fat—an average of twenty-two pounds—from each of the fifteen obese women in the study would safeguard these patients from high blood pressure, high cholesterol levels, high blood sugar and other factors that lead to life-threatening diseases. But the researchers found no such benefits. Removing the fat cells under the skin does not have the same effect as losing the fat around internal organs. As Klein explained:

> Had these patients lost this much fat by dieting, we would have expected to see marked improvements. Even losing a little fat

71

People with questions about weight-loss surgery should speak to a doctor who has experience in the field.

by dieting—far less than what we removed with liposuction— causes significant [health] benefits.... When you lose weight with dieting or exercise, you shrink the size of fat cells, which improves [health].... With liposuction, you remove the number of fat cells, but you don't shrink the size of remaining fat cells.

The study concluded that diet and exercise are "the way to reduce health risks associated with obesity." In his comments Dr. Klein did not condemn liposuction but instead saw the procedure as having cosmetic benefits that "may stimulate people to become more active, which can help them lose more weight or keep it off. If it achieves that, as it often does with people who get liposuction, that is a good thing."[12]

Who Is Helping?

School-based programs to prevent obesity are being publicized currently, but they are not new. A two-year program for children in grades three through six in two Chicago schools was conducted by University of Illinois at Chicago (UIC) graduate students in the early 2000s. The emphasis was on helping the children make healthy food choices. The UIC team wrote brief essays about various vegetables and fruits, which included interesting facts about a specific food and information about its origin. The essays were distributed before lunch, which helped increase the consumption of a particular food, according to a report in *Food Service Director*. Students also learned:

how to make more nutritious snacks such as celery stalks topped with peanut butter and chopped raisins. In fact, snacks received a great deal of attention both years, with good reason. Research showed that during any given day many of the students drank four or five 20-ounce sodas and ate bags of chips and salted sunflowers seeds, all of which could be—and often were—purchased at local convenience stores. So in addition to showing the students how to create more healthy snacks from scratch, the UIC students visited the local stores to find specific snack foods they could recommend.[1]

The second year of the program focused on changing behaviors of overweight girls, who were at high risk for obesity, diabetes, and heart disease. The girls volunteered for the experiment and planned their own activities such as walking more each day and eating fewer high-calorie foods.

In Philadelphia, young people at the inner-city Ecology-Technology Academy (EcoTech) began in 2003 to learn about healthy foods by growing them. Because of their families' low incomes, all the students qualified for free lunches, and ordinarily they would eat evening meals at fast-food restaurants several times a week. But that changed, according to a *Newsweek* report. On an acre of land, students learned how to grow crops, harvest fruits and vegetables, and sell their produce at a low price to people in their community. When school closed in the summer, they also learned how to cook healthy meals. Some students experienced for the first time how fresh foods taste. As one teenager, Johnathan Russell, noted "I never had fresh herbs before. It was store bought all the time. It tastes completely different."[2]

At the other end of the economic scale, in the affluent Ojai Valley School in California, a private boarding school and high school, the students appeared to understand the concept of eating well. Gina M. Fontana, food service director, noted that students at the Ojai School seem to be slimmer than others their age. She explained that vending machines did not offer snacks or soda, only water and

A community program in New York City called Build Healthy Eating and Lifestyles to Help Youth (B-Healthy) that has been operating for years is currently part of a growing movement across the United States known as "food justice," which is based on the premise that healthy food is a human rights issue. Activists believe that unhealthy lifestyles and overweight problems are often linked to the lack of access to healthy food (processed, high-calorie foods are more available and affordable). Food justice activists attempt to address social, cultural, and economic factors that work against healthy food choices. For example, they may initiate community gardens to help low-income families acquire produce. Or they may work with families to change long-held cooking habits of frying foods in lard and using lots of salt—customs that can lead to weight gain and heart problems.

Although most food justice efforts are not well known, activists hope to increase local production of foods and the number of farmers markets. They also want to organize community groups, particularly in inner cities, that will demand healthy foods and reject processed foods from stores and restaurants—small but important steps toward healthy living.

"Let's Move"

In 2010, First Lady Michelle Obama launched an obesity-prevention effort called Let's Move. The program includes a variety of efforts, such as creating healthier school lunches, challenging adults and children to exercise at least five times per week, and encouraging parents to examine their own habits and present healthy examples for their families. Numerous towns and cities across the United States have taken part in Let's Move programs.

An example is Mishawaka, Indiana, where groups of fourth, fifth, and sixth graders participated in a variety of activities for their Let's Move Mishawaka events. Some examples: one group learned how to prepare tasty healthy snacks with the help of a local supermarket; another group learned bicycle safety and the importance of biking

It is important for people to become interested in healthy eating at a young age. These children are helping Michelle Obama take care of the White House garden.

as a great way to stay active and have fun with friends and family. Still another group of students participated in a Fire Prevention Obstacle Course. That is, they crawled blindfolded along a hundred-foot length of fire hose climbing over and under obstacles to simulate the conditions in an actual fire and fire hydrant manipulation.

The city parks department emphasized that "Exercising and burning calories does not necessarily mean a trip to the gym doing aerobics, jogging, or lifting weights. Exercise simply means moving and exerting yourself to get your heart rate up to burn calories and fat. Whether you're playing a game of tag, kick ball, or red rover with your friends, you are exercising and having fun with your friends!"[7]

As Let's Move emphasizes, eating healthy meals is an important factor in fighting obesity. In early 2012, the FDA issued new regulations for school lunches and announced that the new rules would be phased in over a three-year period. According to the FDA:

The final standards make the same kinds of practical changes that many parents are already encouraging at home, including:

• Ensuring students are offered both fruits and vegetables every day of the week;

• Substantially increasing offerings of whole grain-rich foods;

• Offering only fat-free or low-fat milk varieties;

• Limiting calories based on the age of children being served to ensure proper portion size; and

• Increasing the focus on reducing the amounts of saturated fat, trans fats and sodium.[8]

Studies Under Way

Research is also part of the strategy to prevent and treat obesity. The NIH is exploring the many factors that contribute to obesity, such as behavior, culture, economics, environment, and genetics. With hundreds of millions of dollars earmarked for research, NIH hopes to greatly expand scientific knowledge of this complex and many-sided disorder. The new *Strategic Plan for NIH Obesity Research* was released in 2011 (the first plan was released in 2004) and the entire plan or a summary can be viewed online.[9] Some goals of NIH researchers:

- discover key processes that regulate body weight and influence behavior
- understand the factors that contribute to obesity and its consequences
- design and test new approaches for achieving and maintaining a healthy weight
- evaluate promising strategies to prevent and treat obesity in real-world settings and diverse populations
- use technology to advance obesity research and improve healthcare delivery

Whether with the NIH or private laboratories, scientists have long been trying to discover medications that will tackle the obesity problem. In 1994, for example, it seemed that a newly discovered hormone known as leptin could be used to prevent obesity. Leptin, which is produced by fat cells, checks appetite, and it was hoped that it would work as an anti-obesity drug. But scientists have found that in spite of the fact that obese people often have high levels of leptin, their bodies resist it. Thus no leptin-based drug has yet been developed for obesity treatment.

However, identifying leptin prompted some scientists to begin research on other drugs that tell the brain to curb the appetite. Until 2012 only two prescription drugs were available for long-term obesity treatment: Meridia and Xenical. Meridia suppresses the appetite by affecting control centers in the brain that signal how much a person should eat, but in 2010, the drug was withdrawn because of a study that showed Meridia increased heart attacks and strokes.

Xenical prevents the break-down of dietary fats into smaller molecules that can be absorbed by the body, and helps eliminate fat through waste products. At the end of 2003, the FDA approved Xenical for treatment of obese teenagers. However, patients who take the drug are advised to also limit high-fat foods such as pizza and French fries and stay on a low-calorie diet. Even then, weight loss is modest, and side effects, such as lack of bowel control, can be uncomfortable and unpleasant.

In 2012, the FDA approved two weight-loss drugs Belviq and Qsymia. Belviq controls appetite "specifically by activating brain receptors for serotonin, a neurotransmitter [in the brain] that triggers feelings of satiety and satisfaction," Alice Park explained in a *Time* magazine article. "Serotonin is also involved in mood; many antidepressant drugs work by preventing the reuptake of serotonin and keeping brain receptors bathed in the chemical…. [The] drug is designed to seek out only the serotonin receptors that affect appetite."[10]

The other FDA-approved pill Qsymia is for overweight or obese adults who have a chronic condition such as high blood pressure or diabetes. Qsymia is not actually a new drug, but instead is a combination of weight-loss drugs phentermine and topirimate. Phentermine suppresses appetite and topirimate makes a person feel full after eating.

One drug rimonabant, produced by a French company, appeared to be promising in human trials. It is known as a CB1 blocker, and it seems to prevent cravings and may control the desire to eat more than needed. Ongoing trials of the drug involved obese patients in Europe and the United States. In separate trials, the drug helped smokers quit the habit. In addition, evidence showed that the drug was useful in treating metabolic syndrome, the set of disorders that include insulin resistance (which can lead to Type II diabetes), high blood pressure, and risk factors for heart disease. However, the USFDA did not approve the drug because of its negative side effects.

Scientists at Emory University in Georgia announced in November 2012 that after years of study they have discovered what they call "a magical compound." It imitates hormones which are "released in the body after a person eats [and] 'tell' the body to stop eating," according to *Gannett News Service*. The hormone is called

7,8-Dihydroxyflavone and was fed along with a high-fat diet to one group of female mice, while another group ingested only high-fat food. Those taking the compound were much thinner than those who did not consume the imitation hormone. The "magic" did not work on male mice—the compound had no effect on them. However, the Emory scientists expect that their research will lead to a pill or perhaps a tea that will help combat obesity.[11]

Anti-Obesity Advertising

Advertising has played a major role in helping to create awareness of obesity issues and to foster healthy lifestyles. In one TV commercial made more than a decade ago, the screen shows two boys on a beach tossing a football along the shore. Suddenly, one of them makes an unusual discovery: a body part seems to be protruding from the sand. As the second boy approaches, he uses a stick to poke at the object and nonchalantly announces that they've come across a human belly. It was probably "lost" by someone running along the beach, he says. That scene played on television in various parts of the United States as part of an anti-obesity campaign designed by the Ad Council and the U.S. Department of Health and Human Services.

HHS and the Ad Council also helped spread the word about obesity prevention through *Sesame Street* and its supporting nonprofit organization Sesame Workshop. *Sesame Street* characters Luis, Elmo, and Rosita encourage parents to make healthier eating and physical activity part of their family's regular routine—as early as possible in their children's lives.

In 2012, the Ad Council and Clear Channel began a Healthy Habits campaign to address the issue of childhood obesity by promoting Ways to Enhance Children's Activity & Nutrition (We Can!). We Can! is a program of the National Institutes of Health that is "designed to give parents, caregivers, and entire communities a way to help children eight to thirteen years old stay at a healthy

Efforts to combat childhood obesity include programs that encourage regular physical activity.

weight," says its Web site. On the site, there are tips for healthy eating; getting active; and limiting TV, computer, and video time.

However, some campaigns to overcome obesity have become controversial. That was the case in Georgia during 2012. Some videos by Children's Healthcare of Atlanta's Strong4Life campaign are examples. One video with an overweight child tells viewers "Being fat takes the fun out of being a kid," and another print ad and billboard features a young girl with the caption "It's hard to be a little girl if you're not."

Objections about the Atlanta campaign came from public health experts, psychologists, and others who argued that the ads blame the victim and stigmatize overweight kids. Critics contend that fear and guilt might motivate people to change, but there also have to be solutions to problems of obesity. Georgia has the second highest number of obese children in the nation—Mississippi is first. Linda Matzigkeit, senior vice president of Children's Healthcare, told *ABC News* "We needed something that was more arresting and in your face than some of the flowery campaigns out there."[12] Others who support the campaign say that at least the ads are a first step toward public awareness and are prompting people to talk about the issue.

Another controversial campaign in Albany, New York, was initiated by the nonprofit Physicians Committee for Responsible Medicine (PCRM). In early 2012, PCRM sponsored two billboards that warn against consuming cheese and other dairy products because of their high fat content, particularly saturated fat. One billboard showed a man's obese belly beside the words, "Your abs on cheese." The other depicted an obese woman showing her fat thigh with the words, "Your thighs on cheese."

PCRM also sent a letter to Albany's school board asking that schools reduce dairy products in their lunches. A news release from PCRM noted: "More than 59 percent of New York State's residents are either overweight or obese. The figures are even higher in Albany County, where nearly 63 percent of adult residents are overweight or obese. The New York State Department of Health has said that the state faces a childhood obesity crisis, as one in four New Yorkers under the age of eighteen is obese, and the obesity rate for children between six and eleven years of age has quadrupled over thirty years."[13] Whether the PCRM effort led to changes in school lunch programs is uncertain, but Albany and other New York schools have reduced the fat in their school lunches, and like other public schools nationwide have begun to establish menus based on the new FDA regulations.

Healthy Lifestyles

8

Although there are many efforts to help Americans establish healthy lifestyles, some people are taking the initiative on their own to lose weight and be more active. And teenagers are among them. A feature about Christianne (described in the first chapter), who was teased by her classmates because of her weight, makes the point. She told *Choices*, "I went to a nutritionist, I went to a personal trainer, my mother tried to help me, my father tried to help me, but nothing worked." She was determined, however, to control her weight and learned about a weight-loss summer camp, which she attended for seven weeks. With a limited diet and plenty of physical activities, she lost twenty-five pounds. She admits, "I tried to change for other people and I wasn't happy.... When I did it for myself, it made it so much easier." Her advice for overweight teens: "Lose weight for yourself, not for someone else."[1]

Other teenagers admit that over time they have usually eaten whatever they wanted and haven't exercised, thus have gotten heavier. Some say they go home from school and immediately hit the refrigerator or cupboards to find snacks—leftovers, candy, chips, or other items—and nibble away until their parents get home. But once some young people realize that they need to change their behavior and lose weight, they may try to adopt a different lifestyle, eating healthier food and getting active.

Changing is not easy, however, and some teenagers have a more difficult time than others losing weight. Yet determination and perseverance do pay off. A slogan that may work for some is: *Focus on your goal, don't give up, and attain the benefits.*

Family Affairs

There is little doubt that parents can set examples—negative or positive—for their children's eating habits and exercise routines. On the negative side are parents who don't practice what they preach, demanding physical activity for their youngsters but being couch potatoes themselves. Or parents may encourage unhealthy eating habits by the types of high-calorie foods they prepare and the fast foods they eat. Then there are parents who badger their young children and teenagers about eating too much or deliberately humiliate them about their weight. Repeatedly young people tell stories about parental harassment that only adds to the frustration and lack of self-respect that overweight young people experience.

On the positive side are supportive parents who protect their overweight children's self-esteem by pointing out that weight is not a measure of one's worth but could be a health problem. Health is foremost at meal and snack time, and for some parents that begins early in their children's lives. One Washington state couple explained that when their son was born, they felt it was important for their child to experience as many varieties of food as possible while growing up. As a result their son learned to enjoy fresh fruits and vegetables, seafood, poultry, and whole grain foods. Now that he is a teenager, he prefers healthy food rather than junk food most of the time.

Another important way that parents encourage a healthy lifestyle is at the family dinner table. Researchers at Rutgers University suggest a family motto: "The family that eats together and plays together stays healthy together!" A family eating a balanced meal together sets an example that can be followed throughout a lifetime.

For example, Nissa Gay, a certified nutritionist and personal trainer in California, believes she had an advantage because of the healthy eating habits she learned growing up. While she was young, her parents were vegetarians for several years, which "meant eating lots of tofu, vegetables, and brown rice." Then her family modified the vegetarian diet and began to eat fish on occasion, and insisted on healthy food. "There was never any sugary soda pop in the house, and Twinkies were out of the question." Now in her thirties, Gay believes that for teens, "There is no time better than the present to start watching what you eat. Teenagers have the upper hand because they have plenty of time to change 'not-so-good' eating habits." In her opinion, it is important to control portion sizes and to eat plenty of fruits and vegetables which "will give you more sustained energy to get through the day than any artificial sweets. Breads and other carbohydrates are OK when they are based on whole-wheat flour instead of white flour." In short, she says, "Being a teenager is quite hard and there are so many choices to make. By eating right and exercising, the future becomes much easier as an adult. Trust me, I've been there!"[2]

An unusual family effort was undertaken by the offspring of Louis S. Yuhasz, better known as "Big Louie," of Alexandria, Virginia. A morbidly obese man at more than five hundred pounds, Big Louie died of complications from a stroke in 2001, which prompted his adult children to do something about obesity. There was another motivation, as his son Louis explained on the Big Louis Web site:

> *When you or a loved one is obese you learn to live with a prejudice unlike most. You learn to live with stares, humiliation, and people pointing or laughing or asking how you got so 'fat.' We learned with pride to ignore it. They didn't know our Dad and his tremendous heart; they only saw his tremendous size. Our Dad made us better human beings because of his compassion and fearlessness, and he never missed an opportunity to stand up for himself. He rarely missed a day of work in a career than spanned fifty plus years.*[3]

In 2002, the Yuhasz family pooled their own money plus donations to create a scholarship fund called "Louie's Kids," and reviewed applications from overweight children and adolescents to attend the Wellspring Adventure Camp in the North Carolina mountains. The scholarship program has continued, and campers learn healthy living practices—eating nutritious, low calorie foods and exercising. Big Louie's son is committed to the program as his "life's work. "What an experience to see children who are struggling with their size and all the 'baggage' that comes with it to just be able to be themselves in an environment that fosters love and teaches kids 'lifestyle changes' rather than fad dieting. To see the smiles on kids faces as they complete a climb up a rock wall, repel from one mountain to the next, hike 4.5 miles, participate in a sport (as opposed to warming the bench) or find a lifelong friend, as so many of them have, is like no other experience I've known."[4]

Physical Activities

Togetherness is also an important factor in physical activity, such as participating in family ball games or taking family bike rides or walks. To get more physical activity, an increasing number of teenagers and their families are taking part in dance video games that prompt what amounts to an aerobic workout. A popular game is *Dance Dance Revolution (DDR)*, which originated in the 1990s and currently has versions for the Nintendo Wii platform. *DDR* is available in a home version as well as in arcades. The home game includes a plastic dance pad with arrows and a video screen with scrolling arrows. Players choose a song and operate the game with their feet, stepping on arrows on the pad that correspond with arrows on the screen. As the song goes on, players move/dance to the beat, which can increase in speed. One teenager who played the game, fourteen-year-old Natalie Henry, did not know she was losing weight until she went to buy new clothes. She found that her regular size was too large. She eventually dropped from size fourteen to size eight.

Other home video games use motion-sensing technology and a digital camera that allows players to see themselves making karate chops while attacking virtual villains and landing punches in a boxing match. Another game called *GameBike* was designed by two orthopedic doctors and requires pedaling a bike to control action on a video game. Any bicycle can be used—it is mounted on a standard trainer and the bike is connected to a Playstation video console. In racing games that involve cars, boats, motorcycles, or other vehicles, you pedal as fast as you can to compete. Such games are being used not only at home, but also in hospital exercise programs.

Whether or not you enjoy some type of video game that promotes exercise to lose weight, there are other ways to get up and get moving. Swimming, hiking, jogging, skating, and dribbling a basketball are just a few ideas. The point is to get active as the Let's Move program advises.

Exercising with friends can be a fun way to stay fit and healthy.

More Suggestions

Countless health-care professionals, dieticians, and nutritionists provide other recommendations for weight loss and healthy living. Eating right is the major emphasis of the American Dietetic Association, which has a Web site that provides dozens of fact sheets on the nutritional values of various foods. The Center for Science and the Public Interest has numerous ideas for healthy eating, such as a *Nutrition Action Healthletter* with a component that compares "right stuff" food (low fat, low calorie) with "food porn" (high fat and calories).

On the U.S. Department of Agriculture's Web site you can click on an interactive "SuperTracker" that replaced the MyPyramid Tracker. You can track the foods you eat and learn about their nutritional value. The diet score looks at the types and amounts of food you ate as compared to those recommended by the FDA. It also tells you how much total fat, saturated fat (the kind of fat that can lead to heart disease), cholesterol, and sodium you have in your diet. The physical activities score shows the types and duration of each physical activity you did, and then compares this score to the physical activity recommended for health. You can store some information on the site and complete your food intake and physical activity for several days, which gives a better picture of your eating habits or physical activity over time.

Nutritionists and dieticians frequently focus on the importance of reading food labels to determine the calories, nutrients, and other ingredients in a serving size. The serving size is at the top of a label. Below it, the calories and other items are listed per serving. Included in most labels is a list of Daily Values for those who eat 2,000 or 2,500 calories daily. This is a guide to help you get 100 percent of the vitamins and minerals you need each day (from a variety of foods) and to help you cut back on fat, sugar, and sodium (salt) in foods and beverages.

Many young people have realized that adopting healthy eating habits will help them look and feel better.

A quick check of a few products indicates: One tablespoon of Hunt's Ketchup has 15 calories and 4 grams of sugar (in the form of high fructose corn syrup and corn syrup, which are sugars nonetheless). A doughnut may have 14 grams of fat compared to a small bagel with 0.5 gram of fat. There are 190 calories in a cup of canned peaches in sugary syrup, but there are only 110 calories in a cup of peaches in natural juice.

In some supermarkets, nutrients and calories are listed on produce shelves for a great variety of fresh fruits and vegetables. The labels on packaged meats, poultry, and fish indicate calories, fat, and protein amounts. In short, knowing the nutrient content of your food helps you make healthy food choices.

What You Can Do

Along with the recommendations for healthy living and weight loss in this chapter, some excellent advice appears in Jay McGraw's *The Ultimate Weight Solution for Teens*. The book is based on the seven keys outlined in the adult book *The Ultimate Weight Solution— The 7 Keys to Weight Freedom* by Jay's father, TV celebrity Dr. Phil McGraw. In addition, the teen book includes journal-like pages for a reader's comments and answers to personal questions.

With the many healthy living suggestions, it is hard to keep everything in mind. So here is a list, summarizing some of the points:

• Take responsibility for your food choices and physical activities rather than expect someone else to be your watchdog.

• Plan for the long term, not quick fixes.

• Set realistic goals.

• Pat yourself on the back for trying, rather than blame yourself or your heritage for your body image.

• Ask your family and/or friends to support you as you establish healthy eating and exercise habits.

• Go back to your routine and drop the guilt trip if you stray on occasion.

- Limit your time watching TV, playing video games, and using the computer.
- Investigate and choose nutritious snacks; ask family members, nutritionists, dieticians, or healthcare providers for advice.
- Keep a journal to remind yourself about your progress.
- Avoid comparing yourself to celebrities who supposedly have "ideal" bodies but may not be healthy.

Finally, remember an important tip that worked for Christianne (and no doubt many other people): Strive to be healthy for yourself, not for someone else.

Chapter Notes

Chapter 1. What Is Obesity?

1. Denise Rinaldo, "Weight War," *Choices*, April-May 2004, p. 8.

2. Julia Sommerfeld, "Teen Weight-Loss Surgery: Is Benefit Worth The Risk?" *Seattle Times*, March 11, 2005, <http://seattletimes.com/html/health/135178879_obesekids07m0.html> (October 16, 2012).

3. National Institute of Diabetes and Digestive Kidney Diseases, National Institutes of Health, "Statistics Related to Overweight and Obesity," July 2003, <http://win.niddk.nih.gov/statistics/index.html> (June 30, 2004).

4. MedlinePlus Medical Encyclopedia, "Obesity," June 22, 2004, <http://www.nlm.nih.gov/medlineplus/ency/article/003101.htm> (June 30, 2004).

5. "Headed for Heart Attacks? Doctors Fear Obese Teens May Not Outlive Their Parents," *ABCNEWS.com*, June 3, 2004, <http://abcnews.go.com/sections/GMA/DrJohnson/Obesity_teens_health_040603.html> (June 29, 2004).

6. "Teen Obesity," *TeenHelp.com*, 2012 <http://www.teenhelp.com/teen-health/teen-obesity.html> (October 16, 2012).

7. Cynthia L. Ogden, Margaret D. Carroll, Brian K. Kit, and Katherine M. Flegal, "Prevalence of Obesity in the United States, 2009–2010," *National Center for Health Statistics*, January 2012, <http://www.cdc.gov/nchs/data/databriefs/db82.pdf> (October 16, 2012).

8. "Overweight and Obesity," *Centers for Disease Control and Prevention*, August 28, 2012, <http://www.cdc.gov/obesity/data/facts.html> (October 16, 2012).

9. Margot Shields, Margaret D. Carroll, and Cynthia L. Ogden, "Adult Obesity Prevalence in the United States and Canada," *National Center for Health Statistics*, March 2011, <http://www.cdc.gov/nchs/data/databriefs/db56.pdf> (October 16, 2012).

10. Susan T. Stewart, David M. Cutler, and Allison B. Rosen, "Forecasting the Effects of Obesity and Smoking on U.S. Life Expectancy," *New England Journal of Medicine*, December 3, 2009, pp. 2252–2260, <http://www.nejm.org/doi/full/10.1056/NEJMsa0900459#t=articleTop> (October 16, 2012).

11. The Center for Consumer Freedom, "About Us," n.d., <http://www.consumerfreedom.com/about/> (October 16, 2012).

12. The Center for Consumer Freedom, "Food Police," n.d., <http://www.consumerfreedom.com/issues/food-police/> (October 16, 2012).

13. Glenn A. Gaesser, *Big Fat Lies: The Truth about Your Weight and Your Health* (Carlsbad, Calif.: Gürze Books, 2002), p. xiii.

14. Harriet Brown, "In 'Obesity Paradox' Thinner May Mean Sicker," *New York Times*, September 17, 2012 <http://www.nytimes.com/2012/09/18/health/research/more-data-suggests-fitness-matters-more-than-weight.html?_r=0&pagewanted=print> (October 16, 2012).

15. Gina Kolata, "I Beg to Differ; The Fat Epidemic: He Says It's an Illusion ," *New York Times*, June 8, 2004, p. F5.

Chapter 2. Causes of Obesity

1. Amanda Spake, "Rethinking Weight," *U.S. News & World Report*, February 9, 2004, p. 53.

2. Kevin Patrick, Gregory J. Norman, et al., "Diet, Physical Activity, and Sedentary Behaviors as Risk Factors for Overweight in Adolescence," *(Abstract) Archives of Pediatric Adolescent Medicine*, April 2004, pp 385–390.

3. "Even Your Fat Cells Need Sleep, According to New Research," *Sciencedaily.com*, October 15, 2012, <http://www.sciencedaily.com/releases/2012/10/121015170822.htm> (October 17, 2012).

4. Patrick, Norman, et al., pp 385–390.

5. Centers for Disease Control and Prevention, "Adolescent and School Health," June 7, 2012, <http://www.cdc.gov/healthyyouth/physicalactivity/facts.htm> (October 17, 2012).

6. Jessy Troy, "Decrease in Physical Education Participation in High Schools," *fitness blog: always chick, always fit*, December 4, 2010, <http://chickandfit.com/decrease-in-physical-education-participation-in-high-schools/> (October 18, 2012).

7. Kelly D. Brownell and Katherine Battle Horgen, *Food Fight: The Inside Story of the Food Industry, America's Obesity Crisis, and What We Can Do About It* (Chicago: Contemporary Books, 2004), p. 36.

8. Alice Park, "Lack of Exercise as Deadly as Smoking, Study Finds," *healthlandtime.com*, July 18, 2012, <http://healthland.time.com/2012/07/18/lack-of-exercise-as-deadly-as-smoking-study-finds/> (October 17, 2012).

9. Marion Nestle, *Food Politics: How the Food Industry Influences Nutrition and Health* (Berkeley, Calif.: University of California Press, 2003), p. 25.

10. Mary Story and Simone French, "Food Advertising and Marketing Directed at Children and Adolescents in the US," *International Journal of Behavioral Nutrition and Physical Activity*, February 10, 2004, <http://www.ijbnpa.org/content/1/1/3> (October 18, 2012).

11. Alice Park, "Watching TV Steers Children Toward Eating Junk," *healthland.time.com*, May 11, 2012, <http://healthland.time.com/2012/05/11/watching-tv-steers-children-toward-eating-junk/> (October 19, 2012).

12. Dawn C. Chmielewski, "Disney Bans Junk-Food Advertising on Programs for Children," *Los Angeles Times*, June 6, 2012, <http://articles.latimes.com/print/2012/jun/06/business/la-fi-ct-disney-food-ads-20120606> (October 18, 2012).

13. Shanthy A. Bowman, Steven L. Gortmaker, et al., "Effects of Fast-Food Consumption on Energy Intake and Diet Quality Among Children in a National Household Survey," *Pediatrics*, January 2004, pp. 112–118.

14. Inge Lissau, Mary D. Overpeck, et al., "Body Mass Index and Overweight in Adolescents in 13 European Countries, Israel, and the United States," *Archives of Pediatrics & Adolescent Medicine*, January 2004, pp 27–33 <http://archpedi.jamanetwork.com/article.aspx?articleid=485590> (October 19, 2012).

15. Cara B. Ebbeling, Kelly B. Sinclair, et al., "Compensation for Energy Intake From Fast Food Among Overweight and Lean Adolescents," *Abstract, Journal of the American Medical Association*, June 16, 2004, <http://jama.ama-assn.org/cgi/content/abstract/291/23/2828> (October 19, 2012).

16. Center for Science in the Public Interest, "Dispensing Junk: How School Vending Undermines Efforts to Feed Children Well," May 2004, <http://cspinet.org/new/pdf/dispensing_junk.pdf> (October 19, 2012).

17. Carolyn Colwell, "Vending Machines Found in Most Middle Schools," *health.usnews.com*, October 6, 2008, <http://health.usnews.com/health-news/diet-fitness/diabetes/articles/2008/10/06/vending-machines-found-in-most-middle-schools> (November 12, 2012).

18. Ron Nixon, "New Guidelines Planned on School Vending Machines," *New York Times*, February 20, 2012, <http://www.ny-times.com/2012/02/21/us/politics/new-rules-planned-on-school-vending-machines.html?_r=0> (November 12, 2012).

19. Nick Leiber, "Selling Healthy Snacks in Schools," *businessweek.com*, January 13, 2011, <http://www.businessweek.com/stories/2011-01-13/selling-healthy-snacks-in-schoolsbusinessweek-business-news-stock-market-and-financial-advice> (October 19, 2012).

Chapter 3. Health Risks and Costs

1. Weight-control Information Network, "Understanding Adult Obesity," n.d., <http://win.niddk.nih.gov/publications/understanding.htm#Healthrisks> (October 19, 2012).

2. American Diabetes Association, "Diabetes Basics," *2011 National Diabetes Fact Sheet*, January 26, 2011, <http://www.diabetes.org/diabetes-basics/diabetes-statistics/> (October 19, 2012).

3. Lisa Greene, "Diagnosis Diabetes—Special Report on an American Epidemic," *St. Petersburg Times*, April 18, 2004, p. 1A, 8-10A.

4. Ibid.

5. National Institutes of Health, "Treating Type 2 Diabetes in Youth," *nih.gov*, May 7, 2012, <http://www.nih.gov/researchmatters/may2012/05072012diabetes.htm> (October 20, 2012).

6. University of Rochester Medical Center, "1 Million Teens at Risk for Diabetes and Heart Disease," August 11, 2003, <http://www.urmc.rochester.edu/pr/news/story.cfm?id=349> (October 20, 2012).

7. Centers for Disease Control and Prevention, "New Obesity Data Shows Blacks Have the Highest Rates of Obesity," July 7, 2009, <http://www.cdc.gov/media/pressrel/2009/r090716.htm> (October 20, 2012).

8. Susan Blumenthal, "Poverty and Obesity: Breaking the Link," *huffingtonpost.com*, April 11, 2012, <http://www.huffingtonpost.com/susan-blumenthal/poverty-obesity_b_1417417.html> (October 21, 2012).

9. Ibid.

Chapter 4. What About Weight-Loss Diets?

1. University of Pittsburgh Medical Center, upmc.com, "Fad Diets," 2012, <http://www.upmc.com/patients-visitors/education/nutrition/Pages/fad-diets.aspx> (November 28, 2012).

2. Dianne Neumark-Sztainer, Melanie Wall, et al., "Dieting and Unhealthy Weight Control Behaviors During Adolescence: Associations With 10-Year Changes in Body Mass Index," *Journal of Adolescent Health*, May 18, 2011, pp. 80–86, <http://download.journals.elsevierhealth.com/pdfs/journals/1054-139X/PIS1054139X11001765.pdf> (October 21, 2012).

3. Editorial staff, "Nutrition for Weight Loss: What You Need to Know About Fad Diets," *familydoctor.org*, December 2010, <http://familydoctor.org/familydoctor/en/prevention-wellness/food-nutrition/weight-loss/nutrition-for-weight-loss-what-you-need-to-know-about-fad-diets.html> (November 28, 2012).

4. Partnership for Essential Nutrition, "Low-Carbohydrate Diets," n.d., <http://www.essentialnutrition.org/lowcarb.php> (November 12, 2012).

5. "Weight Watchers Announces New Position On Enrollment of Children and Adolescents," March 31, 2003, <http://www.weightwatchers.com/about/prs/wwi_template.aspx?GCMSID=1003161> (October 22, 2012).

6. See <http://health.gov/dietaryguidelines/dga2010/DietaryGuidelines2010.pdf> (October 22, 2012).

7. Ibid.

Chapter 5. More Diet Dangers

1. Kevin Zhou, "The Flawed Media Coverage of Teen Obesity," *Online NewsHour*, September 29, 2003, <http://www.pbs.org/

newshour/extra/speakout/editorial/obesity_9-29.html> (October 22, 2012).

2. "U.S. Weight Loss Market Worth $60.9 Billion," *PRWeb*®, May 9, 2011, <http://www.prweb.com/pdfdownload/8393658.pdf> (October 23, 2012).

3. "Diet Pills Promise Rapid Weight Loss, With Faulty Tactics," *ABCNews.com*, April 23, 2004, <http://www.abcnews.go.com/sections/2020/Living/2020_diet_ads_040423.html> (October 23, 2012).

4. "The French Way to Lose Weight," *WebMD*, n.d., <http://www.webmd.com/diet/features/french-way-to-lose-weight> (October 23, 2012).

5. U.S. Food and Drug Administration, "Dietary Supplements," October 9, 2012, <http://www.fda.gov/food/dietarysupplements/default.htm> (October 24, 2012).

6. U.S. Food and Drug Administration, "FDA Acts to Remove Ephedra-Containing Dietary Supplements From Market," November 23, 2004, <http://www.fda.gov/NewsEvents/Newsroom/PressAnnouncements/2004/ucm108379.htm> (October 24, 2012).

7. U.S. Food and Drug Administration, "Beware of Fraudulent Weight-Loss 'Dietary Supplements,'" March 15, 2011, <http://www.fda.gov/ForConsumers/ConsumerUpdates/ucm246742.htm> (October 28, 2012).

8. "Low-Carb Foods Less Than Meets the Eye," *UC Berkeley Wellness Letter*, January 2004, <http://wellnessletter.com/html/wl/2004/wlFeatured0104.html> (October 24, 2012).

9. Marion Nestle, "Low Carb or Low Fat: Do Calories Count?" *sfgate.com*, August 3, 2012, <http://www.sfgate.com/food/foodmatters/article/Low-carb-or-low-fat-Do-calories-count-3761345.php> (October 25, 2012).

10. See <http://www.cnpp.usda.gov/publications/dietaryguidelines/2010/policydoc/policydoc.pdf> (October 28, 2012).

Chapter 6. Weight-Loss Surgery

1. Dahiya, MD, e-mail correspondence with the author, August 3, 2004.

2. Bellflower Medical Center, "Weight Loss Surgery: A Lifelong Decision," pamphlet, no date.

3. JoNel Allecia, "Trying to 'Hold On' To Weight Loss, Carnie Wilson Discusses Second Surgery," *NBC News*, April 2, 2012, <http://todayhealth.today.com/_news/2012/03/22/10799250-trying-to-hold-on-to-weight-loss-carnie-wilson-discusses-second-surgery?lite> (October 28, 2012).

4. Andrew Seibert, MD (reviewer), "Gastric Banding Surgery for Weight Loss," *webmd.com*, February 5, 2012, <http://www.webmd.com/diet/weight-loss-surgery/gastric-banding-surgery-for-weight-loss> (October 28, 2012).

5. Weight-control Information Network, "Bariatric Surgery for Severe Obesity," *National Institute of Diabetes and Digestive and Kidney Diseases*, June 2011, <http://win.niddk.nih.gov/publications/gastric.htm> (November 12, 2012).

6. Veronica Salotto e-mail to the author, August 15, 2004.

7. Irene Maher, "A Last-Resort Lifesaver," *Tampa Bay Times*, November 26, 2012, p. 1A, 9A.

8. Diana Gonzalez, *CBS News*, "Study Finds Bariatric Surgery Safe for Teens," *ksl.com* <http://www.ksl.com/?nid=157&sid=20891163> (November 1, 2012).

9. Matthew L. Maciejewski, Edward H. Livingston, et al., "Health Expenditures Among High-Risk Patients After Gastric Bypass and Matched Controls," *Abstract, Archives of Surgery*, July 2012, <http://archsurg.jamanetwork.com/article.aspx?articleid=1217291> (November 2, 2012).

10. Anahad O'Connor, "Medical Costs May Remain High After Weight-Loss Surgery," *well.blogs.nytimes*, July 18, 2012, <http://well.blogs.nytimes.com/2012/07/18/medical-costs-may-remain-high-after-weight-loss-surgery/> (November 2, 2012).

11. Robert Kazel, "Insurers Trim Bariatric Surgery Coverage," *AMNews*, April 5, 2004, <http://www.ama-assn.org/amednews/2004/04/05/bil20405.htm> (November 12, 2012).

12. Denise Grady, "Liposuction Doesn't Offer Health Benefit, Study Shows," *New York Times*, June 17, 2004, <http://www.nytimes.com/2004/06/17/us/liposuction-doesn-t-offer-health-benefit-study-finds.html> (November 2, 2012).

Chapter 7. Who Is Helping?

1. Susie Stephenson, "Healthy Kids 101: University of Illinois Nutrition Professor Pioneers Obesity Intervention Efforts in Chicago Elementary Schools," *Food Service Director*, July 15, 2004, p. 34.

2. Peg Tyre and Julie Scelfo, "Helping Kids Get Fit: Communities Are Finding New Ways for Youngsters to Trim Down and Tone Up," *Newsweek*, Sept 22, 2003, p. 60.

3. Gina Fontana e-mail to the author.

4. Kay Lazar, "Urban Renewal," *boston.com*, July 9, 2012, <http://www.boston.com/yourtown/somerville/articles/2012/07/09/how_do_you_measure_success_in_large_scale_anti_obesity_campaigns/?page=full> (November 9, 2012).

5. Janet Lavelle, "Officials Unveil Healthy Works Anti-Obesity Program," *utsandiego.com*, February 2, 2011, <http://www.utsandiego.com/news/2011/feb/02/officials-unveil-healthy-works-anti-obesity-program/> (November 9, 2012).

6. John Byrne, "Coca-Cola Gives $3M to City for Anti-Obesity, Diabetes Efforts," *chicagotribune.com*, November 12, 2012, <www.chicagotribune.com/news/local/breaking/chi-cocacola-gives-3m-to-city-for-antiobesity-diabetes-efforts-20121112,0,7140844.story> (November 13, 2012).

7. City of Mishawaka, Indiana, "Let's Move Mishawaka Program in Our Schools," *mishawaka.in.gov*, January 11, 2011, <http://mishawaka.in.gov/node/1340> (November 5, 2012).

8. United States Department of Agriculture, "USDA Unveils Historic Improvements to Meals Served in America's Schools," *fns.usda.gov*, January 25, 2012, <http://www.fns.usda.gov/cga/Press-Releases/2012/0023.htm> (November 5, 2012). Also see <http://www.gpo.gov/fdsys/pkg/FR-2012-01-26/pdf/2012-1010.pdf> (November 6, 2012).

9. See <http://www.obesityresearch.nih.gov/about/StrategicPlanforNIH_Obesity_Research_Full-Report_2011.pdf> or <http://www.obesityresearch.nih.gov/about/StrategicPlanforNIH_Obesity_Research_Summary_2011.pdf> (November 6, 2012).

10. Alice Park, "Belviq: 5 Things You Need to Know About the New Weight-Loss Pill," *healthland.time.com*, June 28, 2012, <http://healthland.time.com/2012/06/28/belviq-5-things-you-need-to-know-about-the-new-diet-pill/> (November 6, 2012).

11. Gannett News Service, "Possible Answer to Obesity Found at Emory University," *digtriad.com*, November 3, 2012, <http://www.digtriad.com/news/local/article/252783/57/Researchers-May-Have-Found-Treatment-For-Obesity> (November 13, 2012).

12. Lara Salahi, "'Stop Sugarcoating' Child Obesity Ads Draw Controversy," *abcnews.go.com*, January 2, 2012, <http://abcnews.go.com/Health/Wellness/stop-sugarcoating-child-obesity-ads-draw-controversy/story?id=15273638&singlePage=true#.UJaCfmexviQ> (November 4, 2012).

13. "Fat-Focused Billboards Warn Albany that Cheese Makes You Chubby," *pcrm.org*, January 18, 2012, <http://www.pcrm.org/media/news/fat-focused-billboards-warn-albany-cheese> (November 4, 2012).

Chapter 8. Healthy Lifestyles

1. Denise Rinaldo, "Weight War: Growing Numbers of Teens in the United States Are Overweight, and the Problem Keeps Getting Bigger," *Scholastic Choices*, April-May 2004, p. 9.

2. Nissa Beth Gay, personal e-mails and telephone conversations with the author.

3. Louis A. Yuhasz, "About Louie," *louieskids.org*, 2012, <http://www.louieskids.org/louie/> (November 11, 2012).

4. Ibid.

Glossary

ADA—American Diabetes Association

Body Mass Index—A standard for measuring whether weight points to a health problem.

calories—A measurement of the fuel, or energy, produced in the body.

carbs—Abbreviation for carbohydrates.

carbohydrates—Sources of energy found in foods.

CDC—Centers for Disease Control and Prevention.

cholesterol—Fat-like substance in the blood.

diabetes—A disease in which the body does not make enough insulin or does not use it efficiently.

fat cells—Cells in which energy/fat is stored in the body.

FDA—Food and Drug Administration.

insulin—A hormone that regulates glucose (sugar) levels in the blood.

JAMA—*Journal of the American Medical Association.*

legumes—Food plants with pods such as beans and lentils.

liposuction—A surgical procedure in which fat cells under the skin are sucked out with a vacuum-like instrument.

metabolic syndrome—Set of characteristics that can lead to the early onset of diabetes and also heart disease.

NIDDK—National Institute of Diabetes and Digestive and Kidney Diseases.

NIH—National Institutes of Health.

protein—Basic substance of body cells.

triglycerides—Blood fats that increase the risk of heart disease.

For More Information

Academy of Nutrition and Dietetics
(formerly American Dietetic Association)
120 South Riverside Plaza,
Suite 2000
Chicago, Illinois 60606
800-877-1600

American Diabetes Association
1701 North Beauregard Street
Alexandria, VA 22311
800-342-2383

American Heart Association National Center
7272 Greenville Avenue
Dallas, TX 75231
888-242-8883

Center for Consumer Freedom
P.O. Box 34557
Washington, DC 20043
202-463-7112

Center for Science in the Public Interest
1220 L St. N.W. Suite 300
Washington, D.C. 20005
202-332-9110

Centers for Disease Control and Prevention
1600 Clifton Road
Atlanta, Ga. 30333
404-639-3311

Mayo Clinic
200 First St. S.W.
Rochester, MN 55905
507-284-2511

National Institutes of Heal
9000 Rockville Pike
Bethesda, Maryland 20892
301-496-4000

The Obesity Society
8757 Georgia Avenue, Suite 13:
Silver Spring, MD 20910
301-563-6526

U.S. Food and Drug Administration
10903 New Hampshire Avenue
Silver Spring, MD 20993
888-463-6332

Further Reading

Books

Gold, Rozanne. *Eat Fresh Food: Awesome Recipes for Teen Chefs.* New York: Bloomsbury USA Childrens, 2009.

Murphy, Wendy. *Weight and Health.* Minneapolis, Minn.: Twenty First Century Books, 2007.

Owens, Peter. *Teens, Health & Obesity.* Broomall, Pa.: Mason Crest Publishers, 2005.

Sanna, Ellyn. *America's Unhealthy Lifestyle: Supersize It!* Broomall, Pa.: Mason Crest Publishers, 2007.

Wilson, Charles and Eric Schlosser. *Chew On This: Everything You Don't Want to Know About Fast Food.* New York: Houghton Mifflin Company, 2007.

Internet Addresses

Academy of Nutrition and Dietetics
http://www.eatright.org

Center for Science in the Public Interest
http://www.cspinet.org

Choose My Plate
http://www.choosemyplate.gov

Index

A

advertising, 8, 22–23, 25, 38, 40, 49, 83
Amanda, 8
American Academy of Family Physicians, 40
American Diabetes Association, 30
anorexia nervosa, 39, 49
Atkins Diet, 38, 41, 43–44
Atkins, Robert C., 41

B

bariatric surgery, 61, 63, 66, 68–71
B-Healthy, 78
Blair, Stephen N., 13
body mass index (BMI), 10, 12–13, 17–18, 34, 40, 45, 60–61, 66, 70
Brasch, Kendall, 5
Brownell, Kelly D., 20–21
bulimia nervosa, 39, 49
Burger King, 23, 26, 56

C

calories, 16, 21–23, 25–27, 36, 38, 43–44, 46, 51, 56, 58–59, 63, 69, 75, 78, 80, 82, 88, 90, 93, 95
Campos, Paul, 13
cancer, 30
carbohydrates, 41, 43, 56, 58, 63, 89
Center for Consumer Freedom (CCF), 12
Center for Science in the Public Interest (CSPI), 26, 93
Centers for Disease Control and Prevention (CDC), 9, 18, 30, 34

Christianne, 5, 87, 96
Coca-Cola, 77
Comprehensive Weight Control Prevention, 16
convenience foods, 23
Cooper Institute for Aerobics Research, 13
Critser, Greg, 21

D

Dahiya, Shyma, 60, 66, 68
Dance Dance Revolution, 91
diabetes, 8, 17, 30, 32–34, 61, 66, 71, 75, 77, 82
Dietary Supplement Health and Education Act (DSHEA), 54
dietician(s), 22, 45, 63, 93, 96
diet pills and supplements, 49, 51–52, 54–55

E

Ecology-Technology Academy (EcoTech), 75
ephedra, 52, 54
exercise, 13, 16, 18, 20–21, 32, 39, 46, 51, 61, 63, 68–69, 73, 76, 77–78, 80, 88, 91, 95

F

factory farms, 21
fad diets, 38–39, 49, 60, 90
fast foods, 23, 25–26, 36, 56, 58, 75, 88
fat cells, 6, 10, 13, 17, 71, 73, 81

Fontana, Gina M., 75–76
food plate, 45–46
food pyramid, 45, 93
Friedman, Jeffrey, 13, 15

G
gastric bypass, 61, 66
gastric pacemaker, 65
Gay, Nissa Beth, 89
ghrelin, 17
glucose, 32–33, 43

H
heart disease, 8–9, 30, 33–34, 43,
   70–71, 75, 82, 93
Henry, Natalie, 91

I
insulin, 17–18, 32–33, 82
insurance companies, 10, 70
Internet claims, 54–56

J
Jenny Craig Diet Program, 44
junk food, 22, 25–27, 69, 89

K
Klein, Samuel, 71, 73
Kovach, Karen Miller, 45

L
laparoscopy, 61, 63, 65–66
lap-band surgery, 63
leptin, 13, 17, 81
liposuction, 71, 73
Louie's Kids, 90
low-carb diets, 38, 41, 43, 58
low-carb foods, 41, 56
low-fat foods, 25, 43, 46, 56, 80

M
McDonald's, 23, 25–26, 56, 58
McGraw, Jay, 95
McGraw, Phil, 95
Meridia, 81
mesotherapy, 51
metabolic syndrome, 33–34, 82
morbid obesity, 60–61, 69–70, 90

N
National Institute of Diabetes and
   Digestive and Kidney Diseases, 32
National Institutes of Health (NIH),
   6, 12, 32–33, 80–81, 83
Nestle, Marion, 21, 58
New England Journal of Medicine, 9, 71
Newsweek, 75
nutritionist(s), 41, 45, 87, 89, 93, 96
nutrition labeling, 52, 55–56, 58, 93,
   95

O
obesity
   causes, 15–28
   deaths, 9–10, 12, 21, 30
   definition, 8
   economic costs, 6, 20, 29–30, 33,
      36, 70
   health problems, 8–9, 12, 30, 34–35,
      54, 61, 66, 70, 77, 89
   prevention, 30, 34, 36, 40, 63, 74,
      76–78, 80–83
   surgery, 60–73

P
Patrick, Kevin, 18, 20
P.E. classes, 20
Pediatrics, 25
"phen-fen," 52, 54
poverty, 35–36
processed foods, 22, 78

protein, 15, 26, 41, 43–44, 46, 56, 58, 76, 95

R
rimonabant, 82
Roker, Al, 61
Russell, Johnathan, 75

S
Salotto, Veronica, 66
school vending machines, 26–28, 75
serving size, 59, 93
Sesame Street, 83
sleep deprivation, 17
South Beach Diet, 38, 41
Strategic Plan for NIH Obesity Research, 80
Subway, 56, 58

T
Time, 21, 22, 82
20/20, 49, 51

U
U.S. Department of Agriculture (USDA), 27, 45–46, 59, 93
U.S. Department of Health and Human Services (HHS), 12, 45, 83
U.S. Food and Drug Administration (FDA), 12, 52, 54–56, 65, 80–82, 86, 93

V
video games, 21, 91, 95

W
Weight Watchers, 8, 44–45
Weitzman, Michael, 34
Wilson, Carnie, 61, 63

X
Xenical, 81

Y
Yuhasz, Louis S., 90

Z
Zhou, Kevin, 48–49
Zone Diet, 38, 41